Love Unleashed
The Fire and Passion of Poetry

For:

_____

From:

_____

LOVE UNLEASHED

The Fire and Passion of Poetry

ZEMILL

authorHOUSE®

AuthorHouse™
1663 Liberty Drive
Bloomington, IN 47403
www.authorhouse.com
Phone: 1 (800) 839-8640

Published by AuthorHouse 10/05/2016

ISBN: 978-1-5049-7838-5 (sc)
ISBN: 978-1-5049-7839-2 (e)

Print information available on the last page.

Any people depicted in stock imagery provided by Thinkstock are models,
and such images are being used for illustrative purposes only.
Certain stock imagery © Thinkstock.

This book is printed on acid-free paper.

For Information about the Author please contact:
Lyrics Unlimited
www.AttentionRequired.com
(469) 464-9762

Author Contact Information:
Zemill@AttentionRequired.com

CONTENTS

PREFACE

Where do you wanna go with your life? How fulfilling is what you're doing compared to what you really want to do? How intimate is your relationship with love? Do you truly believe in yourself? I pondered these questions for a very long time before I wrote my first book, *Thoughts In Vision-Poetic Works of Love, Life and Inspiration.* Now, with my sophomore literary compilation, I've explored the previous questions and many more. I've looked deeper into the social climate of humanity and found that there are voices that need to be heard but still fall upon silent recognition. Peace and equality are destinies that for many have not yet arrived. Dreams to reach higher lack the grit that real motivation brings and love still begins from a place inside the garden of our fondness for each other.

Love Unleashed – The Fire And Passion of Poetry was written by the pen of inspiration. Every Poem was a thought that came to me either as a lightning bolt to my mind or as a quiet verse into my imagination. Life wrote this book as much as I did and each poem is a story I couldn't wait to share with you. There is truth, there is controversy. Yet more than anything I believe the words are relevant to what's happening in the world today and enlists situations and events that touch all of us. I challenged the library of my vocabulary, and I hope you find the true meaning in the message I'm attempting to convey. I believe Poetry is the *Language Of Expressions.* The Poet sees the glass neither half full nor half empty, but looks at the glass to describe the essence of the water, its fluidity and its refreshing appeal. Life is our canvas, we paint pictures and tell stories in our rhymes. We create images within our verses. We look at the world not only as it is, but propose the beauty and complexity of what it can become.

I'm blessed to be able to share my gift with you. I'm humbled by your audience. I'm thankful for your support. I've had trials and difficult times, we all have. I stared cancer in the face and was blessed not to be given an expiration date. I had to fight through illness, re-acquaint myself with love and use those experiences to continuously move forward and not allow doubt or difficulties to stand in the way of my promise. This is what I wish for you. *Love Unleashed – The Fire And Passion Of Poetry* is about breaking free of constraints. It's about never giving up. It's intimate, romantic and sensual. It's thought provoking and uplifting. It's deep and compelling. Most of all, it is what I am truly passionate about and hope you're touched by these flames of poetry and prose. Live your life to the fullest. Be the promise of your potential for yourself and for others. Be the embodiment, of *Love Unleashed!*

Zemill

ACKNOWLEDGMENTS

We are better working together than pulling one another apart. I'm so blessed to have people in my life that have supported me from the beginning of this journey and have all had a major impact on my growth. I encourage you to surround yourself with positive people and those who share not only your dreams but your vision. The following are people who I just wanna give a special thanks to:

My Brother Byron promised after we lost our mother at the tender age of forty-nine that he would always be there for me. We made a pact twenty years ago that is still intact today. We call each other every week. Not a text or a voice mail but a live conversation. That effort cannot be measured. To his wife Karla, Sister Cooley and all the kids, and there are a lot of them (smile), thank you for your love. To my Aunts Erma Jean and Joyce and my Uncle Charles and my cousins and other relatives, thank you. To my father, thank you for the name Zemill which means *Joyous Melodies*.

To Marion, who continues to help and support me, the events, projects and all that I do. Your dedication is priceless and the job you do does not go unnoticed and you have my sincere appreciation.

To Jonathan and Candice, Trina, Ombrey and my grandchildren, stay the course and never stop driving to be better. You must remain persistent and diligent with all your work and efforts. You have so much life ahead of you.

To Joel B. McCray whose talents as an artist, producer and musician are phenomenal. You had the courage to tell me as a friend that you admired the content of my work, but I needed to work on my performance on the mic. I heard you. I practice daily and will continue to work to live up to the artist that you are.

To Crystal Lassiter, as a friend you told me that I needed to become so familiar with my material, that when I had those 'bumps in the road' I'll keep on stepping and to become so well versed, only the critical me could slow my flow. I live that advice every day.

To Tamara of Tega Creative Studio and Jennifer of Curvy Connect Magazine, thank you for allowing me to showcase my work. Don't forget me when you 'blow up' (smile).

To Penny Sutton, C.W. Whitaker, Carlton McConnell, Shirl Solomon McConnell, D.D. Ingram, Alan Stevenson, Bridget Boyd Monroe, Ed Gray, Dalphne Davis, Dalonika and Harold McDonald, Tommy Jones, Niki, Ella Shaw, Cheryl Smith, Terry Allen, Ora Guy, Curtis King, Chrisila Anderson, Monica Johnson, Etta and Ro, Terri, Youlanda, Shonda, La Sheon, Thero, Terri, Priscila, Keith, Wanda, Renee, Eva Gray Coleman, Lesia & Belinda Ramsey, Stafon Harris-Jackson, Michelle Veazie, Lynne Haze, Sherna Armstrong, Sharon and Christopher Jarvis The Hall Family, The Pope Family, The Vivens Family, Daryle Good thank you for all your support. To Vivian Fullerlove thank you for your positive spirit and support. Attorney David Small and Mentor Jimmy Miller, thank you both for your guidance.

To Mrs. Leatha Evans and Mr. James Jones thank you for your continued support.

To my College roommates Charles Drayton and NFL Hall of Fame running back Eric Dickerson thank you for your continued friendship and support. Eric whenever you come to town I know I'm rolling V.I.P.

To Bobby, Mike and Dennis and all my Roosevelt Classmates (I won't shout out years, smile) thank you for your love and encouragement. Many of you really help lift me up. All my SMU Classmates, thank you.

Dwayne Godwin, you have been great friend and supporter from day one also. You are like a brother and I truly appreciate you and all you've done. Pat Griggs, thank you but I know you still want your cut.

Wes Smooth of Twin Cities Radio Network thank you for the kind words, support and showcasing of my music.

All my Coworkers, Facebook and other Social Media Friends, fellow Poets, all my friends and family, you inspire me daily, I thank you.

Special thanks go to a friend that's no longer with us. Cedric Howard was the consummate friend and brother to me. My first show, not knowing how I would be, bought twenty tickets and he and his wife Tina sat in the middle of the room like proud siblings. I will never ever forget Cedric and his friendship.

CHAPTER 1

SHADOWS OF LOVE

How do you define love, when it's a roller coaster ride of feelings and an exposé on chance? From the beautiful and romantic to the heart clinching frantic, love can be endearing and love can be pain. If you've ever possessed and lost it, you are forever changed. Yet we live to bask in it's glow, and reside in Loves' company. Step into the light, within...The Shadows of Love

My Destiny

If you were not here, I would find you.
Every corner of the earth unveiled.
Every shadow illuminated by the magnetic effulgence
pulsating from the urgency of my instincts quest.

Destiny holds reservations,
for all those who yearn for fulfillment
and accepts the invitation to the
introduction of granted wishes.
The synchronicity of harmonies union,
is an instantaneous phenomenon.

Without you, my life would consist of a never
ending search to capture the immortality
of the elixir and luster only you are able to place
on the completeness of my existence.

The day you told me, I was the catalyst for the
giving of everything you had in your soul,
was the moment my intuitiveness,
told the offering of my reluctance
that you are indeed,
The One!

It Was You

I stopped to think of where I might be
if you were not in my life.
When I set aside my ego and pride
And allowed the purity to flow from your forgiving eyes,
Cascading from the core of your humility,
Was the strength you shared, that anchored my stability.

The fortress laden emotions
Guarded by dragons and haunting ghosts of sentiments lost,
With unfailing tenderness,
You tore down the walls of mistrust
as your patience endured the cost.

A mind, that conceded to be a nomad of time,
Opened up to the possibility,
Of granting loves light to shine.

And at the epicenter, of a hearts revolutionary change,
It was you, who took this beast of aimless wandering,
Laced in kindness, softly tamed.

Mornings' Song

When you said you cared, it became my anthem.
My favorite verse played repeatedly through
the headphones of my temperament.

A wayward soul found refuge as warm-heartedness
showed mercy to a fallen disposition.
A premonition was foretold by clemency,
as your leniency constructed a bridge
transversely over bias's happenstance.

You're here. Nothing else matters.
We'll walk inside resounding skies,
run along beaches of crystalline waters,
wake up each morning to celebratory commencements,
as the sunlight cheers our perpetual unison.

Seasons Of You

You're the oven in the bedroom of our
libidinous Caribbean summer.
The jewel tone colors on the canvas of falls arboretum.
You are the ice that freezes the moments marked
by picturesque encounters of solace in winter.
You're the exhilaration within the
sparkling April rains of spring.
You are the wheel that turns the seasons of my life.
You are the axis by which my world revolves.

Covenant

I refuse to tell you things I don't believe;
I will not falsify or attempt to deceive.
I'm fragmented and fractured and made of tarnished pieces,
Brittle patience with low tolerance adjacent.
No time for foolery and cautious with all things new to me.
My faults have walked in deserts I thought
were barren of scope, until you uncloaked,
The mystery of my misery as I thought
only God saw the best in me.
What you've given my humility,
as your kindness conquered instability,
Was a segue to a source that was
too often devoid of remorse.
Yet you accepted me as I am, your intentions without scams,
And now I can see,
the person I only imagined I could ever free.
Life is no fairy tale and I know
there will be days filled with hell.
But just know at the end the day,
right here with you is where I will stay,
And legions of mountains will never sway,
the love I confess to you this day.

I can't promise that I'll always be there
at the onset of your darkest hour,
But I will not rest until your heartache is devoured.
This is my pledge, this is my promise,
that with you I will always be honest.
Because you stepped into the doorway of my iniquity,
Navigated through the terrain of my insensitivity,
Made cool my moods and gave of yourself without rules,
The heavens informed me that with you I can't lose.
I believe before the world came to be,
Angels assigned you to me,
These vows I petitioned benevolence to decree.
This is my promise, This is my pledge,

That I, will leave you Never, because you, are My Forever.

Serenity

You are the substance, that keeps me grounded
in the chamber of life's gravity,
You alerted the sensors, in the follicles of my anatomy.
The calm in my chaos, the moisture in my rain,
inside your allure, insanity is sane.

Another Time

She sits at the bar she likes to patronize.
To her, they mix the best drinks.
Not looking for company or a dance,
Just searching for a quiet moment,
In the middle of a crowded room.

The ambient noise camouflaged her sighs.
The ice clang in the glass as she stirred so hypnotically,
It was as if she was trying to create a whirlpool,
That would pull her inside the straw,
and whisk her away to escapism.

Surrounded by hundreds of people she's alone.
The breakup of a decade long affair,
Ended by vacated promises, and broken dreams,
that told her to wake up.
Suddenly a tunnel of silence approached her as
she lifted her head to survey the room.
Oh my, her mind screamed. Who is he?
Slowly they make eye contact,
He smiles, she acknowledges,
He says, "Hello," her heart races.

Her mind says why now? No no no!
But her attraction was overwhelming.
He made her smile blush.
He rekindled the warmth in her
That had just left her so coldly.
They connected, on so many levels, he was her saving prince
who encompassed all she felt she had ever wanted.
It was amazing, he was amazing.

Was this a rebound session she asked
herself over and over again?
Could it be a rescue mission by Love?
How could this happen so soon,
After abandonment had just snatched
away her wishful future?
How could this be?

She turns to the bartender asking for the
check and gave him a good tip.
He said "take care, it'll all work out".
She then turned to the engaging Stranger,
now deemed "Mr. Why Now;"
She reaches for his hand,
he says, "How about a hug?"

He squeezes, she exhales the evenings' sadness.
And just before they let go of the magic,
She kisses him on the cheek,
Then whispers in his ear,

Another time.

The Word

Before love became a word, strings from
the harp of hearts, angels heard.
Playing a melody, so engaging and sweet,
sound announced these four letters it would speak;
Declarations of how the depth of
emotions and expression meet,
To convey what connectivity is not able to complete.

I Spoke With Love Today

Astonished and wondering how could this be,
That Love would travel from the borders of tranquility,
And somehow have a conversation with me.
And as Love came closer, imagine my surprise,
as I stood there in awe,
I noticed a tear in Loves eyes.

And then Love asked a question,
"Why does it seem to so many, that I've gone out of style?"
I said, "Love you might wanna have a seat,
this may take a while."
So I said, "Do you want me to be politically
correct, or tell you how I feel?"
Then Love caught me off guard and said, *"Zemill, keep it real"*.
So I said, "We've become a people of instant
want and instant gratification.
We used to talk to each other but now we
have electronic conversations.

I don't know if we value relationships the way we used to do.
Yes there are couples who stay together forever,
but only a few.
We're moving so fast with so much going on,
any sign of drama, you can best believe we're gone.
So now we search for companionship
On sites like Match.com but many just enjoy being single,
they go to work, church, hang out and come home,
and have gotten too used to being alone."
Then Love said, *"I see, very little time for me"*.

Then I said, "Love where have you been there
are so many questions I'd like to ask."
Then Love said, *"I will answer you in truth,
so that the truth may last,"* I said, "Wow."
So I said, "So many people wanna know
why does losing you hurt so bad?"
Love said, *"First of all, I'm a constant, a seed that was planted
inside of you from the genesis of your creation. I'm not seasonal,
I don't walk away, it's people who allow my flame to fade."*

*"When two souls come together in me,
they are bound by the fibers of their emotions.
So when they part, those fibers are torn,
which causes the pain and the commotion.
But those who flourish in my midst,
are bound by an idea called devotion."*

Then Love said, *"Thank you for the time,
I will leave you with this,"*
I said, "I have so much more to ask, this can't be it!"
*Love said, "We will talk again and I will see you soon,
but tell the people this;
Hope and I are close, Time and I have our moments,
and Patience is my best friend.
Also, I hear so many say you have to learn to love yourself,
but do they really know why"?*
I said, "I'll let you tell me, I don't even wanna try."

Then Love blew me away, Love said, *"Before you can share me and what I've placed inside of you to give to someone else, you must be complete and truly at peace with yourself. If you are not whole, then that which is in you born of me is fragmented, and cannot take hold."*
Again I said, "Wow, that's deep." So I had to ask, as Love began to walk away, "Love, how did I get this opportunity? I'll remember this as long as I live." Then Love knocked me off my feet and replied; *"I read your poem, 'Love Is'".*

...I spoke with Love Today,
I...,
Spoke with Love Today.

Unforgettable

Let them tear us apart if you will,
Throw away the dreams and all we planned.
But no one can take away that night in
the fall of our autumn spring,
When I held you and felt your heart beating
With the dance of a thousand drums.

Each breath exhaled,
Blew wind songs that engulfed the shores of eternity.
In that parenthesis of time,
We painted our souls in the halls of
unforgettable recollections.
We carved our love, on the transcripts of forever.

Reflections

Gazing across the waters, surveying paintings without colors,
Chaperoning empty love songs of
those pretending to be lovers.
You were the melody and the music,
You rewrote the lyric sheet of my ambitions and infused it.

Sirens ring, through the portals of my memory,
Drawings without images Lost in the dust of hollow chivalry.
Before you, pride had abandoned a soul filled with canyons,
Overshadowed by brittleness holding on to doubts expansion.

I breathe the air you exhale
You were there when promises failed.
A smile so loud, it erased dark clouds.
A presence so soft, more than beauty allowed.

You were my magic, I your gadget,
You flipped my switch you knew all the buttons to hit.

My Isis, my Cleopatra, the lingering in the vibrations
Of our before and after.
Celestial filled temptations, succumb to love-jones migration.
Upon my chest your head would rest.
Always giving more, no option for less.

Reflections of a time,
When a simple touch was divine,
A million to one odds you beat,
Removing the bitter, you made my life sweet.

Reflections broken in sections
You were the piece
That made my puzzle complete.
Familiar and different
Yet refreshingly unique.

You're the ultimate dichotomy
The pleasure of pain deep inside of me.
The remote that changes the channel of my moods
The tranquility in the storms that's allows stillness to soothe.

With me flawed and not worth it
You made love feel perfect.
Taking my minds unfurnished catacombs,
Delivering joy
And making my thoughts your home.

Eclectic and electric what you give is measured in metrics.
To be precise, you are both fire and ice.

For you, my Concert in the park,
I solicited Elysian Fields,
Was granted the release of barren wistfulness
Upon my final appeal.
My first and last chance
More than an Interlude of Romance.
The element that propels my seasons to change.
The oxygen in my air,
the pendulum of my state-of-minds care.

Reflections of a time,
When a simple touch was divine,
A million to one odds you beat,
You removed the bitter,
And made my life sweet.

Reflections broken in sections
You were the piece
That made my puzzle complete.
Familiar and different
Yet refreshingly unique.

Penitence

I wish you didn't love me,
Because then the jubilation you long to share
would not be escorted by turbulent despair.

I wish you didn't miss me,
for then the resonating silence in this hollow place,
would not have painted pictures now erased.

I wish I hadn't kissed you, because then my lips wouldn't
know the sweetness of your spice that tastes like the
pleasure from biting into a mountain of irresistible flavors.

Why did you let me hold you? When you knew
your embrace would insatiably chase,
rainstorms of passion across my longings landscape.

Why, why, why,

Did you have to find me?

Acquitted

No matter what it takes
I don't wanna be your mistake.
Thoughts congested, emotions arrested,
feelings reflective, honesty rejected.

The sanctum of our refuge now confused
as *What was* plans its escape
and *What could have been* surrenders to *Too late.*

You wanted something else, I had nothing left,
Why asked for the truth, *Realization* said, "I see."
Finality consulted *Unanimous,*
and released *It's Over*
to *Free.*

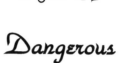

Dangerous

We can't keep doing this.
The magnetism between us is too hot
and undeniably enticing.
You're a magnet to my virility.
The fusion that synthesizes our connection is so
irresistible it cannot be regulated or constrained.

I shouldn't be here. You shouldn't answer my call.
We both know where this ends up.
Why is it so easy to risk it all?
Is it the stealing of each-others forbidden
instruments of amorous erotica?
I know there are genuine strands of affection between us,
but when we went our separate ways we said no more
drowning in the steaming romp of lasciviousness.

I can't stop you, I can't turn away. All you have
to do is say my name and I'm on the way.
It's not just the two of us anymore,
there are others to think about;
The ones who say it's us they can't do without.
I admit I've gotta quit.

We can't pretend the bond doesn't exist,
Quarantining our interaction is the only
solution that makes sense.
I can't see you and you can't call me,
this thing between you and I is too luscious a treat.
Let's not play with matches, I know it's incredibly
tempting and stirs such a licentious rush,
I can't do this,
We're too dangerous.

Caught Up

This is not what you wanted.
You never thought you'd be in this place
But here you are in disarray,
And the illusions of rainbow years have gone astray.

You gave your best, never less
But it wasn't enough, just *Empty Lust*.
I feel your frustration, your prides constipation,
as your mind confesses this is a bad situation.

You got Caught Up, they made you smile, and before you know it,
You're picking out bathroom towels.
You were tired of being alone it had been a while,
you were looking for *Yellow Brick Road* and got *The Green Mile*.

You shared bank accounts, stocks and bonds and even your 401k.
Your friends told you to stop,
You only knew them for 3 Days!
But you said it was *Lightning In A Bottle,*
Wedding March Gears were in full throttle,
To walk the aisle on *This Is It* rose petals,
And for nothing else would you settle.
You got caught up!

Now your muted screams can't find notes to sing.
Sitting on the porch of disbelief,
The interrogation of your *Common Sense* lends no Relief.
Dejected because you swore this was a divine collaboration
But don't know how in the hell you got
Caught Up,
In such a bad situation!

Complicated

In the beginning you said everything was cool,
but somewhere along attachment road you changed the rules.

After the physical, ideas beyond mystical,
began suggesting and requesting,
extended interludes for nesting.

What began as a casual encounter speared by mutual attraction,
produced addiction led actions,
which spared no expense in exploring hypnotic satisfaction.

So now as the period of enchantment has suddenly passed,
on an affair condemned not to genuinely last;
because it was noted upfront we were not
in a rush to claim a lasting endeavor,
but you ignored the truth, thinking you were so clever,
your Stuff could magically change the name, of a love called Never.

How did we get to this plateau entitled twisted and jaded?
It's because you flipped the script, the minute our soirée
was consummated, enter illusions of how a tailored affair
can be escalated, we have now checked into,
Motel, Complicated.

Well here we sit, at the table of obsolete,
words spoken with intervals and sentences incomplete.
You trying to hide your texting because
our conversations have gone sour,
bored to hell at dinner because each minute feels like an hour.

Levity has dissipated, and now faded in the air,
accompanied by periods of silence,
the remnants, of a failed and calculated dare.
Not only are we not on the same page,
we're not even in the same book!
You're no longer the person that lowered
That Bait that got me lasciviously hooked.

We said no pressure we said we could be friends,
but as always sex changes the plot
and a new agenda begins.
What started out as mellow and sweet,
is now exposed as pretentious deceit,
with emotions headed for cover and retreat,
as smiles no longer have a place to sleep.

You said you'd be ok, all you wanted was
a little play, which I knew at the time
was just something to say, until you could place
conditions on a consummating lay.

Now here we are, on the bridge of commitment,
misled by intentions on the shores of resentment.
Not because there're no feelings, not because I don't care,
but because you manipulated the moments
like a poker player who gambled on a stare.

I get things change, I get that sharing your
body and soul you deem an investment,
but sometimes lovers are like game show contestants,
where a chance to win has no guarantee,
rolling the dice with your feelings,
is Heartbreak Jeopardy!

And now you play your trump card, you tell me
you want matrimony or don't call you anymore.
Forcing me to choose between you
or that *Its Time To Leave Door.*
I was ok, right up to the point,
you gave me that ultimatum, until that demand,
I thought just maybe we had a chance,
then reason spoke to my mind and asked,
How you gonna blackmail romance?

Relationships built on lies and schemes end up
as nightmares and unfulfilled dreams.
We both have to want, desire, feel and be
at the same optimal place in our life,
Nothing we have going on between our
Legs is gonna make that time right.

In what millennia will we see,
you can't make somebody love you,
Or change them into who or what *You* want them to be.
Real love evolves naturally,
Kindled by molecular sparks known as chemistry.

If there's a change in the game,
The new rules have to be urgently communicated;
Because if we're delusional about what we have,
That's how things become... Complicated!

Crazy

I know you're no good for me. My 'denial' cross
examined my 'reason' and after deliberation
'raw attraction' found me guilty and
sentenced me to the insanity of love.

You said you wanted a good man,
then you said you were bored,
After getting all you asked for, his reward is to be ignored.

He said he wanted a good woman,
the preverbal "lady in the street and a freak in the bed",
but no matter how many chandeliers you swing from these days,
he'd rather hang out with his boys instead.

You want him to have a little dog in him,
makes you feel excited and protected,
but when the real hound comes out, you call the pound,
now he's spade, neutered and rejected.

You say his stomach has gotten too big,
he tells you he doesn't like any of your wigs.
You used to have conversations at dinner.
Now you're texting under the table saying you're
typing something you're trying to remember.

You said you needed more affection and attention,
then you get too much,
so enter the needles of dissension.
But now it's all about you needing your space,
and what you had in common is now an empty place.

You want what you can't have, you need a
challenge because if they're too nice or easy,
you don't value those people very much,
but now you're unhappy because you're being
mistreated and the one you didn't want,
now you can't touch.

Can't let go but still holding on,
sidestepping the truth that something's very wrong.

Good girls like bad boys, bad boys like good girls who
like to be bad, why do so many songs sing about
"I lost the best thing I ever had"?

We always think the grass is greener on the other side,
something new will always make your head turn,
Until you jump that fence and slide on the ground,
and find out its artificial turf, it's not real so you got burned.

I think we only think we know what we want. I question
if we really do, based on all the evidence, there's nothing
to support my theory is false, so it must be true.

Forget about being sensible, this is my conclusion,
though the details are ridiculously hazy,
I think it's just a game, and we're all plain crazy.

Listen

How can you hear me, when your ears are muted by the
compelling predisposed inference of cross examination?
The truth is of no use, because from my confession you
deduced your summation; albeit received like a blind
man being interrogated by sign language translation.

Rather than just sitting there waiting for your turn
to weigh in on "what you think you know",
Why can't you not presume me guilty
and let your assumptions go?

If you've already made up your mind before I even speak,
I would argue that's like trying to tell you
something important while you were asleep.

In other words, to have a real conversation
the door has to swing both ways,
The mind has to be open to hear what's being expressed,
if we're telling the truth, let the defense rest.

But most of all, if your focus is only on your rebuttal,
Critical details are tuned out and often come up missing,
It's astonishing what you can truly discover,
when you earnestly listen.

Do You See Me Now?

Against the Bentleys and riches that blinded you,
I couldn't compete.
But I was willing to lay never ending faithfulness at your feet.
Security without ambiguity from the
everlasting to the everlasting,
Like that GEICO car Insurance
Every 15 minutes, whatever I had was yours for the asking.

I was the one who made you laugh,
Opened your doors and pumped your gas.
Collected those couchie coupons like
they were going out of style,
And whenever you needed someone to talk to or listen to ya,
It was my number that you dialed.

I'm not the guy who made you cry,
Yet I inhaled your every sigh.
If my heart was blown apart,
And CSI, was called in to examine the shattered pieces,
The synergy of our chemistry would still be distinguished.
Under that ultra violet light, evidence of my devotedness
Would still be detected,
And traced back to this man you once rejected.
Beneath their microscope at the molecular level,
The forensic report would read, "No one else
could have ever loved you better".

No devil from purgatory could've broken your spell,
I would've entered the gates of hell, to pay your ransom
Or make your bail, then wrapped you up in a cool blanket,
As I carried you from your cell.

I've been standing here all this time,
But you just kept pushing me to the back of the line.
We had something, even you said for
us there would come a day,
But then the dollar signs and all the fancy material things
Hooked and took you away.
He abused your feelings in ways that were absurd,
While I stood on the ledge of your every word.

I do not relish seeing you in pain like this,
I came when you called, because your call,
I tried never to miss.
Across your contentment he drug a raging plow,
And at this moment I get why your pride has collapsed
and your humility must reluctantly bow.

But in the midst of your brokenness
As you ask yourself how,
I just wanna know,

Do you see me Now?

I Don't Know Why

A once cherished thing called us,
Now searches to fill moments of empty rosters,
Because of the emergence of a love,
that's been exposed as an imposter.

Too often you made things too complicated,
Reciting conversations not remotely related,
To the reruns of an affair that's been edited and jaded,
By the turmoil between us,
over a union that has painfully faded.

In the twilight of our dawn,
Subtle echoes from our hearts chanted silent sparks,
That pierced dried emotions like polished darts.

Where there used to be laughter,
Is but an express sequel to loves hereafter,
With empty life lines thrown, to closed arms for capture.

Now in the mirror of my memory,
are tales filled with a host of simile.
Escorted by seasonal misery,
the smile that once softly enchanted me,
Now rests in the abyss, of my forbidden tears history.

And I don't know why.

Remembrance

I remember our last dance, when the only thing
between us was the thread that moved between
the choreography of our embrace.

I remember the song that serenaded our senses
beyond the borders of tranquil waters amid the
sequence of the stirring waves beneath our skin.

I remember our last kiss, a rush of intimate bliss,
as we stood simultaneously within the silence of sound,
as if only you and I existed in the land of Love Eternal found.

I remember you, and in that instance of infinity,
the melodies adorned our serenity; your beauty, your smile,
clinching my inclinations like the wonders
of the ancient river Nile.

Yes, I remember that moment.
Yes, I remember you, most of all,

I remember us....

Ode To A Lost Love

Post cards to an address no longer found
Return to sender notice from an affair now extinct
As worthiness struggles to rebound.

Thoughts of delectable inseparability,
Broken and decayed by colloidal inconsistency.
Commitment morphed into resentment
as we became hell bent,
To depart from a love we felt was heaven sent.

Looking at the all the possibilities
Now humbly accepting the frigid realities,
While coming to grips with the fact
that all the evidence shows,
You've moved on,
And I've gotta let you go.

Bittersweet

Within the catacombs of my solitude
are murals of abstract fountains raining encrypted petals,
accompanied by inquisitions,
inquiring why your unfrequented company,
is no longer celestial harmony.

As yesterday's sorrows notify unanticipated tomorrow's,
Recollections subdivided in sections,
crisscross a kaleidoscope of subtle
kisses now turned near misses,
and a love that once epitomized *Enduring and Unique*,
is now labeled by an exit sign that reads.....*Bittersweet.*

Indeed

For those moments I cross your mind,
and the warmth of that thought makes you sigh,
as you feel my fingers caressing your hair,
making your heart smile because now I'm there.
Wherever you are, my imagination sees,
the bond between us is unbreakable... Indeed.

Clairvoyance

You are the constant in my atmosphere;
creating captivating commonality to parallel realities,
Allowing you to be transcendent in an instant,
reinforcing your commitments
To touch me like no other,
As I willingly surrender my independence.

Your words piercing and poignant,
check mating my desires as if you were Clairvoyant.

Raindrops

Is it in the rain, I see your name,
that calls to me for your touch to claim?
Are the drops that fall against my window really
knocks on the door of my anticipation?
Or are they the racing of two hearts stampeding
toward intense torrid fluidity?
I say yes, to all the raindrops suggest.

Not Enough Time

I never count the days, hours or minutes,
For in your company, time is endless.
The tone of your voice and your soothing touch,
Resounds in my pulse, like a stampeding rush.

Every quarter hour gives way to every half hour,
With you seconds pass through like the
cooling of a chilling shower.
The invigorating gleam causes the hour glass to scream,
Don't let the sand run out
On our picturesque mosaic scenes.

The hands on the clock pause and stop,
To extend the way, we make moments holidays.
We borrow a little light from suns beaming might,
So the stars that shine on us,
Slow the turning of day to night.

Every movie reel we fill, sets a panoramic collage
To our unions infinite appeal.
And as we hold in our hands, the very air that we breathe,
There's never enough time,
To fulfill, our timeless needs.

Enjoyment

What we have is not platonic.
You are like the combo meal
I order at Whataburger or Sonic.
Double meat with cheese
Strawberry Malt and Tater Tots,
Mustard on the side served piping hot.
You're all of that nonstop.

My Steak & Shake Beans Baked,
We go together like ice cream and cake.
We enjoy each other so much
I feel like I have to repent,
Because my thoughts of you have been
Naughty and nice ever since,
That one little kiss that night at your door,
we couldn't let go, like being at Ponchos
We both raised the flag for more.

All I'm saying is this, we can't deny
Though we try, we go together
Like Beanies and Weenies
Like eggs and toast
Like a peanut butter and jelly sandwich
with ice cold milk as a toast.

So what do you say we do this thing?
Have dinner at Pappadeaux's
Or just go out for some wings?
You know you wanna
And I do too
I gotta taste for some pancakes
How about you?

I Like You

You make me laugh. I don't know how you always do it but
you do. You're funny, in a joyous kind of way. And oh yes,
thanks for not telling me you heard my stories a million times.
You just grin and act as though you're just now
hearing it the moment I'm telling you
for the umpteenth time.

And another thing, I like you. Have I already said that?
You're fun to be around and just hang out with.
You have a loving and kind spirit. They really don't make them
like you anymore. Are you sure you're from this planet?
You tickle me. Seeing you happy makes me happy.
You are the honey in our company.
And by the way, did I tell you, I really really like you? Oh, ok.

You know what else? I gave it some thought,
and did you know that loving someone is one thing,
but when you like someone, just being in their space is cool.
Anytime, anywhere. And oh yeah, one more thing,
smile if you like me too.....Ah yeah,

I knew it!

I knew it!

When I Look At You

To gauge your beauty would be like measuring a moment in
the now, against the enormity of perpetuity. Oceans would
ask the moon to change the force of its gravitational pull,
so that the crystal sand like beaches I see
in your eyes would remain full.

Before words became a language, attempts to describe
your aura had been met with anguish. Not even the
dictionary enlists an adequate enough vocabulary to
connect the cerebral and the pulmonary with the projection
of your image that to me is simply, extraordinary.

Bach, Beethoven, Picasso and Di Vinci,
painted a Monet on the canvas of a symphony,
to capture the radiance of your smile with imagery,
so the annals of time could record
the reflection of your symmetry.

When I look at you from a distance or even from across
the room, the antenna of my peripheral registers a SOS,
because your pheromones telegraphed your perfume;
alerting my sight to what I was about to see,
a women sculptured by the hands of God
because your glow is heavenly.

When I look at you I euphorically appreciate,
the process of how the pupils in my eyes dilate,
sending signals via the retina to translate,
the light rays through my cornea to punctuate,
the refraction signals
my brains sensory nerves have to articulate,
to project the high definition vision
only your splendor can panoramically generate.

I'm satiated in a glance that endlessly reigns supreme,
at the footsteps of your delight shall I proclaim you my queen.
The sight of you is insatiable,
the universe dwells on your face as does the shimmer of
star light that shines upon the Mediterranean Sea,
I am your Pharaoh and you're my Nefertiti.

When I look at you I see,
When I look at you I see,
When I look at you, I see..... Love.

Endearing

If time did not exist,
Osmosis would suggest to my consciousness,
to petition the heavens, and bring birth to creation,
A unit of measurement that defines the
foreverness of your splendidness.

Contact

You spoke to me in silence,
Calling my name without words.
You touched me without contact,
And I absorbed your signal and heard.
Everything your impulse conveyed,
Your eyes spawn the topography,
Where our futurity is laid.

Simply Said

I wanted to write you a poem,
expressing thoughts you say I'm unwilling to share.
My hesitancy rests not with reticence,
but wanting to say words to you that
transcended beautiful yet commonly used endearments.

I wanted the verbalism to be profound and when you
read the phrases and the verbose articulation,
the sheer translucency of our exchange
would titillate the very marrow in your bones.

But words I thought no longer evocative or sufficient,
are suddenly reminiscent,
and I'm enamored how when Simply Said,
can only be realized greater, when dynamically shown,
more than a modest interchange, can subtly be made known.

Who am I to suggest, to say *I Love You* is not enough to say,
when my deeds and declaration both show it's true?
A wordsmith may record the sentiment more elegantly
but the authenticity of sincerity in
corresponding these three words,
is an institution of expressivity.

Therefore, I humble my pen to this end.
Simply Said, "I've loved you, since the genesis of time began.
And every day I love you, all over again".

CHAPTER 2

COMPELLING THOUGHTS

Life's challenges require us to be aware of social events that impact our lives. The ups and downs of emotions. Questioning why the world turns counter clockwise to ones' image of peace and equality. Compelling Thoughts looks at the dynamics of love and life via an open dialogue.

Let's Talk

I've got a challenge for you.
Let's have real a conversation.
Without technology, street psychology or
unintended words with apologies.
I'm talking about live interaction, face to face engaging,
without a phone, robot speaking drones,
laptop, notebook computers or custom ringtones.
Just me looking into your eyes feeling what
you say the way we used to do.
Not just sitting thumb punching on our cells,
which might mean you're not paying attention;
Then my reply is spelled "WHAT THE HELL"?

These silicon communications and Morse code abbreviations,
have undermined the art of stimulating conversation.
When you're in the "moment" and that chime
rings signifying you got a notification,
an instant message or a reminder,
its kills the mood and it's like you're wearing a blinder.
Then you say it's an email and you had
to get back to the sender,
implying a cyber-sent message is more important
than any "real words" that person right across
the table from you could surrender.

Why are we typing when we could just as easily talk?
We've now made Ebonics electronic,
and the true meaning of our thoughts,
are implied and often lost.

I don't wanna have to be limited,
or autocorrected on some touch screen,
I wanna see how you look and not be
interrupted by some "new age" ring.
I may feel like whispering in your ear or
blowing soft kisses down your neck,
But I can't because you're playing tic-tac-toe
with your bleeping spell check.

I get we live in a busy world and we all got a lot going on,
But when we're together it's nothing
like conversing one on one.
You working on a big deal, family or something urgent I get it,
But quality time is hard to find so when
we're together let's get with it.

Because there are certain special messages that
can't adequately be conveyed in a text,
Like seeing you respond with a shimmering smile,
Because you heard and felt words you never want to forget.
So let's talk, just you and me, put the devices down,
And let the conversation run free.
Then lay back after we've loved the night away,
Having pillow talk together alone,
And not with that third party, we call our phone.

Don't Judge Me

It begins when you see me;
Random thoughts of ignorance start creeping.
Fear of what you don't know, no evidence to show.
You're no better than me based on
the perception of you I see.

You prod and you stare, bitterness in the air,
All because of who and what you think I am.
Driven by a society whose hollow scope,
suggests if I'm different, I may use dope.
By stereotypical images you are provoked,
Because you believe everything on TV and
the Internet is real and never a hoax.

A closer look at the ballistics will show
if you check the statistics
There is good and bad everywhere if
you truly wanna be realistic.
You don't know me, you can't see my soul,
do you only go by what you've been told?
And what about just me as a person,
not a star just an everyday Joe?
I have talent I have skills and personality,
or is that something you care not to know?

At the end of the day, I just long to be free.
Regardless of my race, color, gender or beliefs.
I'll let you do your thing and you let me do me.
And when you look at the world that way,
what a better place it would be,
When we stop judging one another,
Based on blindness, we can't see.

For The Brothers

This is for the brothers who go to work every day;
No pimping, sagging or bragging,
just striving to live a life worth having.
We give props to the rich and celebrity dads,
now let's honor the men of the working class.
Not living the High Life or part of a Highlight,
But being the father, his kids wanna be like.
This is for those brothers

The ones teaching their children and
reinforcing what they learn in school,
Helping them with their homework,
and the importance of rules.
That it's not all about the flash and the cash,
but the legacy they leave when their time has passed.
He shelters his baby girl from a cold and cruel world.
Hips her to the tips of how young males like to trip.
He'll talk to her about being a lady,
he'll counsel her on romance,
Encourage her individuality and for her self-respect,
always take a stance.
He's making a better way, for children to run and play.
Bringing home the bacon and working to change all wrongs,
Then taking care of his lady as soon as he gets home.
This is for those brothers

Not the players or shot callers, High Rollers flaunting dollars.
But that dude you can trust when times get tough.
The one you might often take for granted,
because he's always there,
the one who will listen when no one else seems to care.
He's more than a lover, he's your best friend,
the one you count on, when others pretend.
This is for those brothers

Fighting the good fight, a champion of right.
Not for the glory or headline story that's not who he is,
he's the guy that always keeps it real.
I know you say he's hard to find but
maybe you're not looking,
With your heart, spirit and mind; because oh too many times;
Your eyes will show you lies,
And what you think you see,
is only what you wished it could be.
This is for the brothers, who get overlooked,
Because he didn't get all the check
marks you listed in your book.
Now you're screaming about how some "dog" did you wrong.
You could have had John, but you choose Tyrone.

This is for the brothers working to make a change,
To a system of injustice so we're all treated the same.
Not boastful and full of rhetoric,
but behind the scenes and making sure the courts get it.
He knows he has to work harder even when he's smarter,
Than those who hold him back because
of the color of his skin,
But maintains his dignity and respect,
and for that, will battle to the end.
Knowing the strikes he already has,
but not using them as an excuse, though few understand,
The duality of reality that plagues the black man.
What he has to deal with every single day,
Just to be recognized and significant
in a "Dream" called the USA.
This is for those brothers

Who take care of their homes,
accept responsibility for their actions.
Does what he says he'll do, so his word has traction.
He's gonna stand in the storm, keep his woman from harm,
Make her smile in her sleep because
she knows he doesn't creep.
This is for the brothers who you let slip by,
And then gave everything you had, to one who made you cry.

For the mentors and leaders who nurture young minds,
To the ones that will answer the call when you need them,
To come fix your flat, or give you quality time.
He opens the doors, completes his chores,
does all the little things too often ignored.

This is for the brothers,
who humble themselves to the belief of a higher power.
And his ego doesn't have to be stroked
every hour on the hour.
He's confident and secure in himself, he stands up straight,
Understands the value of time,
so when he picks you up he won't be late.

This is for the brother, who's not undercover,
He's not trying to hide things he
doesn't want you to discover.
He tells you up front, he's not a pretender,
he doesn't play the games,
Where the rules can't be remembered.
He walks the walk and talks the talk,
his loyalty can't be stolen, compromised or bought.

He stands up for himself, he stands up for you,
And no one is gonna tell him what he can or cannot do!
He doesn't envy the rich or the one who appears to have it all,
He's just doing his thing and in his own space standing tall.
This is for the brother, that's just a good guy,
Extraordinarily Ordinary and keeps his head to the sky.
This is for those Brothers

Happiness

Dance in the streets
Say hello to someone
You always wanted to meet.
Open your eyes
Look beyond the now.
Be at peace with you.
Plug into your wow!

Live like you sing in the shower!
Fast forward then rewind each hour.
Look ahead, face every day
As a brand new test,
Find the spot inside your life,
That taps into your happiness.

Because You Are Woman

This is for the women who know, you are the center of
relativity in all that exists, and without you,
the void created by your absence, would produce a chasm
within the landscape of our continuum so vast,
it would reduce the width and depth of the Grand Canyon,
to no more than a single grain of salt beneath
the shelves of the oceans floor.

This is for the mothers who nurture their young,
teaching their children lifes lessons
and how ones' adulthood comes.
For the women who at the end of the day
battle through traffic,
sidestep havoc, pick up the kids from school,
make dinner and get them to practice.
What is innate in you comes from a place
that bends time and curves space,
how you can know what your child is feeling
behind the look on their face. Loving without conditions,
for your family you sustain courage
beyond what words can mention.
For your own you would give your all,
you're there to lift them up when the winds of malady call.

And for the women who make your own way,
confident in who you are
and not influenced by what others say.
Your walk, your talk, the way you dress
and how you carry yourself,
there's no mistaking your worth,
because class tapped you on your shoulder at birth.
Your individuality may cause some
to perceive a certain morality,
Yet the beauty in you, supersedes the visual in view,
and the outside inspection is often met with corrections.
Although you're aware that it's nice
to be aesthetically pleasing,
the inner you must match what spectacles are seeing.

Professionally, monetarily and without charity,
there can be no ambiguity
and this must be stated with clarity.
Unlike men, who begrudge broken hearts that mend,
you open up to give love more than a second chance.
Because your ego is not the guide that drives
whom you decide to give openly, what we try to hide.
This goes out to the women who forgave the lies.

This is for the women who don't do jealousy or messy,
squash the petty, yet remain ever ready
to take on a world that might see you as meek.
Then stand and take notice
when you are nothing close to weak.
For if that hand hits that hip and your
neck is in a retractable motion,
you're about to take it to the streets
and finish what started as commotion.
But only if you're pressed
and your respect is tagged with neglect.
You're a giant in the boardroom, superhero on Wall Street,
a mother, a sister, a lover, and a beast between the sheets.

To the women who find a way to make it,
when life suggests her struggles can no longer take it,
yet somehow you're still able to smile,
because giving in to the turbulence is not your style.
You get up every day, you look in the mirror and say,
"I gotta do what I gotta do, this is just another doorway
to my blessing that I gotta run through."

This is for the women who say with or without a man,
on your own two feet you will stand,
because you demand the best and won't settle for less.
Success is so much sweeter when shared by two,
but you'd rather not partake in the carousel and just do you.
You don't hate on others you just do your own thing,
you help those trying to get to where you are,
instead of trying to steal a name.

You take the noise inside the screams,
flat line the drama and make sound serene.
For your ability to juggle all of lifes tumbling balls,
for your intrinsic intuition you inherently call.
Know this to be endlessly true;
until the life-force that enables oxygen
to convert the serum of breath
that allows me to breathe vanishes,
I will love you, even more I will respect,
honor and applaud you.
I will always pricelessly hold you in high regard,
especially those whose forgiveness goes beyond the compass,
of the extra yard.

This to you is my salute, no one can refute.
Because of the emotional strength,
you often courageously have to summon,
the munificence of your giving that makes you uncommon,
but most of all for being incredibly irreplaceable,
because, you are woman.

Darkened Light

Silent echoes scream to penetrate the residue of silence
only to find refuge in the shadows of obscurity.

Pastures of emptiness await a landslide of bitterness,
driven by the brokenness
Of what could not be held, yet still desired,
while only entertained by rejection.

Looking back has no future;
today finds relief bankrupt of resolution.
Only tomorrow extends a glimmer of reparations.
Only the dawn brings restitution and dissolves
the fragments of a falling stars request.

Midnight is the threshold of new beginnings.
It is in the light of new mornings that
darkness fades amid radiance.
It's the road forward that marks the path to another chance.
The first step, ...is boldly letting go.

I Am A Poet

A gentle breeze colored in pastels,
a whisper of light that moves thoughts to sail.
Within the mural of my creativity was
placed this gift known as poetry.
I am but a vessel commissioned to transcribe spirited thought,
When the melody of the message is received in purity,
The translation to imagination
Is then never lost.

My journey is my truth, my scars fill my verse
The streets have been my navigator
Enlightenment and knowledge guided me to self worth.
I am a poet.

My words paint pictures
Like the brushes of Monet on his beautiful Vanilla Skies.
When you open the ears of your heart
The words will pull back the veils from your eyes.
For within the metaphors you will find,
awareness beyond the sequence of time.

I write of love, I write of life
And all things in between.
My rhymes introduce the seasons,
And carry mellow waters down endless streams.

I write to lift you up, I write to inspire dreams,
To lay passage ways to possibilities,
And give your mind cause to sing.

This is more than what I do this is who I am.
I live and breathe the words I write.
With a panoramic phrase of imagery,
I bring color to the night.

Emotions concave, pain is swayed, travel light years in days,
To these words I am a slave.
When my thoughts run free I'm compelled to be me.
For with each syllable that emerges from my paper and pen,
Born are the jewels of this gift, God placed in my hand.

I am a poet.

I Just Wanna Know

(This Was Her Question)

Why did you take my soul, bury me in violent holes,
Pushing me to the brink of collapsing control,
Only to hide the pain, in my minds bitter cold.
I just wanna know.

Mental starvation supplemented self conscience frustration,
Placing my life on full alert,
by how I undervalued my self worth.
Then the day came, when overwhelmed by shame,
Shrouded in neglect abandoned by loves network;
I declared my future a failing test.

Yet as I stood at the doorway of oblivion, about to fall prey
To self inflicting decisions, wondering in the end,
How my story would be mentioned.

And then I heard the voices of angels beginning to sing,
It was the melodies of my children that
resonated in me a change.
God's amazing grace, through them called out my name,
I found refuge in His benevolence,
And I will never be the same.

You hurt me yes and almost tore me down,
But where once I was lost, now I am found.
Beyond the sadness, peace in my heart has come to be,
And the pains of your remains are now set free.

Now the only question I have,
Knowing, the answer is because He loved me so.
Why God chose me to save,
I live for Him to know.

Nappiology

You are a woman of strength, style and cool,
You are independent and you set your own rules.
The confidence in your walk says smooth
And the psychology of your Nappiology
Expresses the freedoms you choose.

Maybe it's the swirls, the curls, twigs, afros or braids
Or could it just be the texture I feel as my fingers
Travel through the softness of your silky wool-like maze?
The way you wear your hair, so many crave,
Your Nappiology is sexy and with you I am amazed.

You are natural you are real,
there is even something mysterious
About your dauntingly striking appeal.
Sometimes when you brush your hair, I see the waves,
And from the shower to the time you walk out of your door,
The aroma of your look lingers and stays.

Other styles are fine;
I enjoy the many looks that women bring,
Yet yours says so much about the person you are,
And so often it's about stepping out
and doing your own thing.
How you wear your hair, is more than a fad,
it's a statement of truth.
Your Nappiology represents your individuality,
Your Nappiology is you.

Night Moves

It is the night that hides the light.
As intrigue is fatigued searching for shadows unseen.
Lurking in places, abstract faces, interpretation gated.
Mystery elated, because its stealth like
moves are clearly shaded.

Secrets

I wanna tell you something but I can't. Because if I told you,
I would no longer be. I'm dying to let you know how everyday
there's a stampede raging on the cusp of my correspondence.

The threshold of my tongue is tingling to expatiate
utterance of dialogue that expounds upon a testament
only you are able to receive. But I can't.
I want to so badly, but it's important that I remain captive.

Because if I'm released, I will cease to subsist.
The discourse of our symposium cannot be rendered.
Its modesty is to safeguard you and those affected
by my connection to them and hidden conjecture.
It's imperative that I'm concealed so
that I may remain, unavowed.

Moreover, if I told you, not only would I no longer exist,
but what I swore to protect, would instantaneously be
exposed. Don't ask, because I really can't tell you.

Smile For Me

Would you smile for me? Yes you, right now, just smile.
There's only you and I and these verses inviting you
to imagine what you will. Let the words tickle your
fascination as the pages keep us company.
Join me, lets take a trip; come on... :)

When was the last time you did something out of character?
That's not you? Well why not? How about the time you
had so much fun laughing and frolicking the day away just
doing what you were into and it was only you? Ah hah,
yes you remember that thing you did and were so sure
nobody would know? And it was good too wasn't it?
Hmmm yes! I'm not telling a soul, your secret is safe with me;
but it was off the chain right? Yeah I know.
That made you smile didn't it?

The words warm you, they take you to faraway places,
and they remind you of the impressionable chapters
in your life and to reminisce. They give hope to possibilities
of the days to come. The words allow you to escape.
They endear happiness. It is you who blows the winds of life,
that sets sail to these sheets of wood and ink.

So come on, I see those cheeks heading north.
You're getting closer, the picture is clearer,
you're getting nearer,
you're almost there, you can't hold back any longer,
here it comes now... :) there it is!
I so love when you do that.

I feel your wonderment skipping across the syllables
asking yourself, can he see me? Yes, I can see you,
through the verbiage as your eyes
waltz across theses phrases.
And I hear you reading to me as I also hear you saying
back to me why don't I smile? As you're asking yourself
can you really be having this conversation? Even so,
you ask yourself again, is he smiling? And I say, yes I am.
And I can tell you truly that I am :)

Because you're here. You're holding and listening to my
thoughts in your head; and if only until the second you
reach that last sentence, I have your undivided attention,
because you chose me to open and explore. And now I'm
saying to you how much I enjoy you and want you to stay
forever and ever and ever, just so I can see your smile,
when you hear the reverberations of the chimes in your mind.
Then I share your sigh, because when it's time to go,
you don't wanna lay me down.
And I don't want you to leave.

So come on, one more page, how about another poem?
Either way, just once more, smile for me; come on and smile,
...mmm yes, there you go; I see you.........oh how I love your :)

Thankful For The Whoopings

Parents didn't play back in the day,
even the neighbors threw belts your way
Now we did have madness going on,
but being illiterate, rebellious and thug life
Weren't glorified, and weren't happening in our home.
There were a couple of rough necks in the
hood that always broke the rules,
And yes there were always a few kids who acted a fool.

And you better be back in the house,
before that street light catch you out,
Because you knew that if you didn't,
your butt was gonna be turned out!
But you'd better not have your teacher call your house
And say that you were cutting up in class.
Because that walk home was gonna be like the Green Mile,
Cause you knew how your parents
was gonna whoop your azz!

Parents didn't play back in the day.
They would tell you in a minute,
I brought you in this world, I'll take you out!
And I'm sure there's some of you who
know what I'm talking about
They would tell you to stop sniffling or get out,
before I give you something to pout about!
You ain't paying no rent, you better go sit down
somewhere and act like you got some sense!

And if you acted like you wanted pitch a fit,
They'd say buck up if you want to,
I'll give you a back hand lick!
I can still hear my mother saying you ain't paying no rent,
You better act like you got some sense.

Or how about when you were playing
in church or falling asleep,
And your grandmother told you to straighten up.
But you rolled your eyes, like you didn't like what she said,
That was the very time that her, the deacon and the usher
Would pop you upside your head.
Parents didn't play back in the day.

I grew up in the hood; my mother was a single parent,
And she did a great job of raising three boys.
Yet there were times when we needed a man's hand,
To teach us the ins and outs of what the world would demand.

But when my mother worked 3 jobs,
my grandmother who had so much love
Strength and wisdom,
would always be there, to pick up the slack.
Whatever went down, She always knew what to do.
These days grandmama,
might be in the club on Thursday night,
in a mini skirt ages 28 to 32.

I'm not saying whether that's good or bad,
I'm just saying these are different times.
My generation had kids young too,
But I feel our parents were stronger and
wiser and to me that's the truth.
And crossing your parents was something
you really didn't wanna do.
For every offense there was a consequence.
Not even the late great Johnny Cochran
could build a good enough defense.

That being said, I will never forget the
last whooping I ever got,
I was beat down with everything but the kitchen pot.
It was for branding my little brother,
Wait a minute, don't' ya'll act, like I'm the only one
who did something crazy to their little brother?
Come on now!

You see my parents, my family and the neighbors,
Were preparing me for the struggles of life.
They were teaching me responsibility,
values, discipline and respect.
They had already been through what I hadn't seen yet.
But I was too young to appreciate the lessons,
because I didn't fully understand.
But today I'm thankful for those whoopings,
Because they made me a better man!

Rise Black Man Rise

For your heritage and for your people,
for your legacy to which there is no equal.

For our daughters who need their fathers,
to show her how she should be treated.
She is a beautiful queen,
and in the arena of life, she solely is undefeated.
That she can be what she chooses and never
let her self-confidence change,
Don't tolerate or accept being disrespected
Or called out of her name
That the length of her skirt does not measure her self-worth,
For she is among the most precious of
creations to ever walk this earth.

Rise Black Man Rise!

For our sons who need guidance when
dealing with lifes riddles,
To fight for the right to not lose their life,
over a bag of skittles.
That he is a King, encourage his dreams,
Teach him the essence of what being a real man means.
That dignity and respect comes with success,
And impressions are made by the examples you set.

That jail is hell,
And there is no honor in showing off his tail.
But with hard work, persistence, drive and education,
He too can become, the president of a nation,

Rise Black Man Rise!

For our women who have truly gone through so much,
And for those who still long for a real mans' touch.
This is not about the sex nor am I
suggesting who you should love,
But every now and then,
A Sister just needs a hug.

Yes she can make her own way.
Yes she knows how to get things done,
But she'd still like to have somebody she can hold on to,
Until the morning comes.

But most of all she wants us to be honest and attentive,
Respect and support what she aims to do.
Be the one that she can count on,
For whatever she's going through.

Rise Black Man Rise!

For yourself and for your people.
For your legacy to which there is no equal.

You are more than a gladiator, touchdown maker,
hoop star magician
Or home run technician.
You are science, you are music,
An intellectual and enthusiast.
You are the seed that formed all life.
You marched to a dream,
That made freedom right.

For those men who are handling their business everyday,
taking care of their families.
Especially those working to save our sons,
We applaud and salute what you are doing,
In understanding the job that needs to be done.

This call goes out to those on the side lines,
For the sake of our children
And all the lives we must touch,
We need your help, get in the game,
It's time to man up!

Rise Black Man Rise!

For your heritage and your people,
for your legacy to which there is no equal.

Rise Black Man Rise!

The Elusive "It"

How can I find you when I'm oblivious
to who and what you are?
The precursors to the search to unearth a
singularity whose rarity is a velleity undefined.

An obscure identity only recognized when
chance encounters intimately,
What I didn't know I wanted instantly,
wrapped in a veil of anonymity.

If you're not there, I can't hold on to another.
If you're not present, wants are not discovered.
You are the bridge that links whether to stay or go,
without your existence there is no show.

Success is defined by whether I have you or not,
Enthrallment has no merit, if your sign says stop.

You are elusive and conclusive, an anomaly that commonly,
Is the single most engaging factor,
That binds our attention to a transcendent fix,
The "what if" and "whatever will be"
Are all predicated on the incomparable,
"It".

That Little Black Dress

There's nothing like elegance sashaying
across the floor as the music plays.
Or seeing you step out of the car as all eyes raise.

Sophisticated and sexy, every tantalizing step arrests me.
Causing my sight to pause, rewind and then reset,
as I zoom in on you, in that Little Black Dress.

Hot and vibrant, full of pizzazz, you make a
fella wanna buy you twelve tanks of gas.
Bare oiled skin or charcoal shear hose, pumps that thump
with telegenic energy is how your portrait flows.
Laid to highlight your figure,
or made with a free flowing flare,
bodacious is the aroma of your mystique
that scintillatingly sparks the night air.

Those legs that beg, attentiveness to be fed, as patrons drool
sitting on the edge of naughty minded seats, anticipating a
glimmer, a glimpse or revealing peak. Only to be disappointed
because exhibition is not your style, you just like the way it
looks on you, as cognizant engrossing thoughts will run wild.

Masterfully you move, your pace enchantingly smooth.
The countenance of onlookers as you leisurely stroll by,
causing conversational interruptions
as your hemline straddles your mid-thigh.
You are amazing, desirably enticing, encouraging Notice,
to yell and confess, "I suspect mischievous notions tag along,
when you hit the town in your Little Black Dress".

The Good Times

I remember when Roosevelt, Carter, Kimball and SOC
was the hottest ticket on any block. Sprague Stadium on
a Friday night, was one big party and we did it right!
The band was jamming, drill team prancing,
cheerleaders dancing and in the stands were all kinds of antics.

Now it wasn't me, but everybody could
smell puff puff and pass,
from all those getting high on a little grass.
Brown paper bags with Boones Farm Strawberry Hill,
Old English 800 and MD 20/20,
Whatever your flavor was, your neighbor had plenty.

I remember the girls wearing hot pants,
back outs and those sexy smoking micro miniskirts,
and if she had some boots on with that outfit
she looked like Cleopatra Jones and
knew how to make it work.
Now I'm just keeping it real,
if you were trying to holla at a sister,
you had better check your grill,
because if it was jacked up she didn't have nothing to say
but *keep it moving player and go somewhere else and play.*

I remember smothered pork chops that would
melt in your mouth they'd be so tender.
And how did your mother make ten
dollars last the whole week,
And then take an old loaf of bread and
make bread pudding taste so sweet?

We made syrup, mayonnaise and grill cheese sandwiches
with that big block of government cheese,
we didn't always have what we wanted,
but momma got us what we would need.
But boy when you got that pressed ham,
summer sausage and that roll of paper filled with bologna,
it was on and popping baby,
because we were about to get down on it.
We'd cut a thick slice of that meat,
put it in one of those heavy black cast iron skillets
until it bubbled up, burned and fried,
and just before it popped,
we'd flip it to the other side.

I remember playing dodge ball, kick ball and tag you're it,
good kids played hide and go seek,
but we played hide and go get it.
We didn't know Spanish but we all were a little mannish.
There was Galaga, Centipede and Ms. Pac Man at the Arcade,
and it was nothing like an ice cold glass
of your mom's grape Kool Aid.
We didn't have iPad's but we had etch-a-sketch,
all we needed was to be outside
and our imagination did the rest.
We ate neck bones and Honey-Combs
and loved trick or treat,
made capes like batman and superman
from your mom's old sheets.

And then there was the beat-downs, with ironing cords,
extension cords, switches, brooms and belts,
and when your mother and grandmother finished,
your butt had nothing left.
And every single kid, told the same ole' lie,
"I'm not gonna do it no more!"
All that did was add extra licks
and you tried to sleep where it wasn't sore.

You see back in the day parents demanded respect,
you said yes sir and yes ma'am,
And was happy to get breakfast, lunch and
dinner out of one can of spam.
They weren't trying to be your friend,
you talked back to your mother, and your life could end.

I remember long before we shopped at Nordstrom's,
Neiman's, Macy's and Lord and Taylor,
it was Levine's, Sanger Harris and even the Army Navy.
Now all these kids have to have Reebok,
Under Armor and Jordan's to fly higher,
we had Pro Keds, Chuck Taylors and went
to Payless for some P F Flyers.

I remember real music when songs had meaning like from
Stevie Wonder, Cameo, Con Funk Shun, Gap Band, Maze,
Luther, The Barkays, The Commodores and The Temptations.
We chilled with The Emotions, Patty and
Gladys on Greenville Avenue
at a place called the Filling Station.
We had Bernard II, Popsicle Toes, Studio
67 and RJ'S BY The Lake,
Throw on some Parliament or Dazz Band
and the whole room would shake.

I remember when two dollars' worth of gas
would have you rolling all night,
We just had good clean fun with our friends
and nobody was looking for a fight.
It was all about just having a good time,
living for the weekend
And just happy to see the sun shine.
We got high on life, but didn't lose our minds.
And people can say whatever they wanna say,
and that's all just fine,
but to me, nobody had it like we did,
those days we called... The Good Times.

Trust

Trust is a must
That has to be discussed.
But more importantly,
It's imperative this narrative
Is woven into the fabric of who we are,
And what we are to one another.
The comfort of our connection must be continually displayed,
If the permanence of us is ever to be made.
The assurance of knowing, my being is safe in your hands,
Is the pedestal by which, the premise stands.

What's Next?

From Voices Inside The Madness

This poem is not about a revolution, devoid of solutions.
Nor is it the rhetoric of some angry black man.
These words come from the Voices of
people living inside the Madness,
Not those judging from some place in the Stands.

Let us be clear; there's no justification for
unprovoked violence or stirring up a fight,
But just because you say it's legal,
doesn't always make it right.
"You want me to respect your authority
then respect me as a man;
When you abuse the position you've been commissioned,
you've crossed the line in the sand."

This is how it is from sunrise to sunset,
I'm living in this Hell, so tell me What's Next!"
You wanna know My Story despite what you've heard,
Then Listen to what I see, In My own words.

Shot down, Hands up, can't breathe, in hand cuffs,
Death by strangulation, left up to interpretation.
Can't vote, Future choked, not sad, just mad.
Because you tell me, I didn't see what I saw,
I didn't hear what I heard,
Jury acquits, No time served.

Not often for "Them" but mostly for "Me,"
Somebody explain how Freedom is free!
When I leave my house will Fate get me home?
Or will I be just another number that life dialed up wrong?
Poor Guidance, sanctioned silence, desperation,
jail migration, nowhere to run, fallen sons.
The law is raw and Not Enough has Changed,
for People of Color with Unknown names.
This is how it is from Sunrise to Sunset,
I'm living in this Hell, so tell me What's Next!

I don't make the Guns, I don't slang cocaine,
why is Death my Paradise and my Pain?
You say I must Learn, you say I need Knowledge
When Survival is my Course, and these Streets my College.
Racially profiled, harassed for no reason.
If I dress a certain way,
Just Cause becomes open season.
If I'm Innocent of a crime, Why do I have to cop a plea?
How hard did you Search for the Truth,
before inequality convicted me?

Every day is a Struggle, every minute I Hustle,
I'm Trying to hold on, but the Pressure is Long,
Too many kids dying, too many done wrong.
You wanna know My Story, despite what you've Heard,
Then Listen to what I see, in My own words.
This is how it is from Sunrise to Sunset,
I'm living in this Hell, so tell me

What's Next!

They Lied

You've been led to believe that you couldn't achieve,
So a cell block number is waiting to be redeemed.

Wanting you to cross a line, drawn by a struggle
That hasn't been kind.
Bullets fly, children die, mothers cry,
In a war zone so close, you can only question why?

But here's where the transcript of fortune can change;
Fate did not mark you at birth to live a life of the insane.
They lied

They lied when they told you you'd never amount to nothing.
That you had no chance when all you
could do was sing and dance.

They lied when they said you weren't smart enough.
They had no idea how your self-worth could strut!
Too many times, it was implied by prime time,
your face wasn't suitable;
Now it's universally acknowledged that Black is Beautiful!

They didn't take into account you're the blood line of Kings,
That the mother of humanity was your Queen!

They lied when they said you have no choice;
that only prolific failure was in your voice.
Let's 'Choose' to tell the whole world,
emphatically, that's not the truth,
Don't settle for being a casualty,
just turn your self-esteem loose!

Yes there are difficulties when you're not working with a lot,
But don't let your measure of Ascent record,
That Effort and Urge were not on one Accord.

Don't let them be right, Refuse to be a Statistic!
Your mind has to drive Self-Doubt aside!

And as the Naysayers convene,
under estimating how hard you Tried,
Let them witness your celebratory ceremony,
And without question know,
They Lied!

Until...

When will the day arrive when I can look outside,
see that life has survived humanities continued divide?

How can unrest, surpass its test,
when too many remain oppressed,
by those with so much who ignore and reject,
those surviving with less?

There's no confusion in the solution,
equality must be our preamble and not a delusion.
The rhetoric from those in positions
of power have all gone sour
as frustration escalates in an attempt to terminate,
hopeless mindsets that feverishly collaborate.

As long as injustice rules the lanes of our streets,
the quest for peace, will never find sleep.

In Search Of Peace

What do our lives hunger for more than nourishment?
A phantom ideal, a request, an appeal to walk in
the audience of lifes most precious zeal?
It is the search for peace that's driven to be unsealed.

To bring into order the arrangement of disarray,
those maladies muddled by messiness,
for the ending of volatile madness we must pray.
For the infirmities and travesties and yes the disbelievers,
who perpetuate propaganda petitioning to deceive us.

If you do not believe in what I do,
then don't bow your head, if hatred harbors your allegiance,
then one nation under God dare not pledge.
If my rights offend you, I will not apologize,
but do not underestimate my intellect
by politically misrepresenting the law in disguise.

How can one man get twenty five years to life
for a five pound bag of weed?
And another does no jail time for destroying thousands of
lives embezzling millions, boasting pure gluttony and greed.

From the ashes of revolt was this country born and hundreds
of years later tyranny resides in holographic form.
Through the oppression of disingenuous interpretations
of our justice systems scale,
which weighs disproportionately on those of color
whose lives too often collide in hell.
Yes factors abound, circumstances resound,
and where poverty exists, poor representation is found.
First comes stress, then demotivation, frustration,
isolation, anger, escalation, broken communication,
irreverent reputation, all bricks of combustible situations.

No I'm not advocating violence, history may record
battle field victories, but rarely tracks the residual misery.
Only in self-defense do I say raise a protective hand,
yet if you lived with brutal distrust,
discrimination and hopes life line
was devoid of irrigation,
the well of patience only runs so deep,
until reality screams for self-preservation.

The problems are systemic, degradation is epidemic.
We must call to order a hearing, of all earths nations
starting with our own, there are too many wars in
monetarily challenged neighborhoods right here at home.
There are no microwave remedies, as the rift between
the haves and have nots grows ever more wide;
where there's exponentially segregated wealth and education,
degenerative mud will continue to slide.

This is our challenge, rooted deep beneath the caverns
of our constitutions premise of opportunity.
Change can only be manifested
when cemented in unbridled unity.
The obliteration of ignorance can be our ignition,
this is the single greatest priority of our mission.
The statutes of Liberty's torch,
must shine from the apex of privileged way,
to the deepest crevice of despair laden streets,
delivered by the Sincerity of Real Hope,
is where we begin our search for peace.

Can We Start With This?

Why do you call each other names but get mad if other
people do the same? It's not cute, and don't you think
it's time to move on? Let's lay to rest a word where
all its connotations are negative and degrading.

I'm not trying to preach a sermon about a word
that's imbedded into our culture, but there's nothing
special about being called anything that denotes
you are worthless, no good or less than human.

And how can you be so proud to promote the
wretchedness of a word that for some,
describes what you are? Still others say,
the word describes how you act. Don't you feel it's time
our vocabulary raises its bar
and gets "that whip" off our backs?

How about "Champion"? How about "Star"?
Not just for those on TV or in the movies,
but in the communities where you are?
The perception of our people in so many eyes
comes down to what the media "may" surmise.
It's also related to what only a segment
of our population does,
by which all of us shouldn't be judged.
We're not all in 'helicopter shots' circling from above.

Many of our people contribute so much
to life, health and science.
We financially impact all aspects of the lives we are living,
Bringing positive input and influence in all that we're giving.

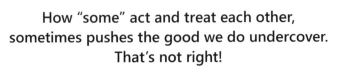

How "some" act and treat each other,
sometimes pushes the good we do undercover.
That's not right!
I get everybody that looks like you is not your brother,
but everyone that doesn't, isn't trying to cause you trouble.

We are so much greater than what we see on any Movie
Screen, TV, Radio, Sport, Court or Street. We're gifted in
all phases of where Life and Social Contributions meet.

We hail from the mother land of all mankind.
We are descendants of Royalty. Do you really know your history,
and what that lineage of Kingliness means?
If you knew where you came from,
maybe your actions would better show,
the Heritage of your Ancestry, on today's Societal Row.
Be what you were born to be, a person of Nobility
and not what your conditions look at you and see.

Your environment and your upbringing does play a part,
but countless thriving people had bitter and difficult starts.
Let's not put and pull each other down,
that would be a historical start
where new pride could be found. Let the Sovereignty
of your Ability define what your Reflection will see.

We can accomplish so much,
when we unitedly lift one another up.
When we support each other's efforts,
not just because we look the same, but because of the quality
of work or service we offer, you're proud to sign your name.

We're linguistically talented enough, not to need this
stereotypical symbol as an artistic crutch.
And as hard as it is to believe,
we can begin a revolutionary elevation to our esteem.
With the invalidation, of one simple noun,
adjective or verb, however it's used,
though some will resist change and call the idea absurd,
can we choose to abolish, the infamous N-Word?

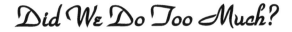

Did We Do Too Much?

There's a question that we don't often want to touch,
yet it is a subject we must openly discuss.
First of all let me say I'm excited about where
many of our young people are headed
I'm just concerned about those who appear lost,
Because by making their lives easier than we had it,
We've made many of them socially soft.

The words that follow are not meant to offend you,
Nevertheless, I must speak the truth,
if not, the words have no use.
I'm merely posing what I feel is a poignant question.
The court of public opinion is always
open and is now in session.

Have you ever wondered did we do too much for our kids?
By wanting our children to have it better than we did?
So we tried to rid their lives of struggle,
but in turn did we raise them up,
In lifes pretentious imaginary bubble?

How can you appreciate the good and
you've never known the bad,
or articulate the difference between what
brings you joy and what makes you sad?
How can we let a teenager foolishly take the lives of others,
And his defense be both insane and insultingly clever,
Basically they said he was so rich, he didn't know any better?

This case is extreme but do you get what I mean?
We had discipline we had respect, not just for our parents
But for every elder we met.
We threw paper routes, mowed yards and
young girls worked in department stores.
Now you stampede through glass on holidays
to "give" your kids what they want,
And trample over people while breaking down the doors.

Children run your house they make the rules,
and scold "you" if you're late picking them up after school.
I didn't grow up like that. My mother would
beat me down if I wanted to clown.
We were taught to work for what we had,
everything had a price.
We had to earn our way, we had to learn to fight.
If things come too easy or I give you everything you want,
How will you learn to value things,
or deal with those who don't?

There's no substitute for experience,
I'm not able to shelter you from all the worlds' pain,
At some point you gotta know if it's cloudy outside,
you may need an umbrella, just in case it rains.
I see parents who give their kids "all of this";
they gotta have the most expensive "that".
Then they talk to their parents like they're crazy,
and wanna call the law if they get smacked.

I'm not saying you were wrong,
I'm not saying all our kids tuned out bad,
But so many young people are emotionally weak
and dysfunctional, and to me that's sad.
We were taught wisdom, we were taught
to appreciate everything we got,
This is a generation of 'entitlement',
if we did do too much, when does it stop?

The Truth

(The Principal To His Freshmen Class)

All of our lives we've been told we can make it if we try.
I believe that's true, yet stipulations do abide.
Nothing will be given to you unless
those before are able to give it,
If not you better bust your butt
And if you are a procrastinator you better quit it.

What's your plan, what's your goal?
Do you have talent to run for the gold?
Is it in your heart, how bad do you wanna win?
If you can't answer these questions,
You've lost before you began.

Life is hard, the real world is not a game.
Its not, win the war with a joy stick
And on the high point scorers list is placed your name.
What are your skills, how will you live?
Until the time comes when you exist greater than your bills.

Enjoy your youth, yes, experience life
to the fullest of its thrills!
But when the *'school bell of your life rings,'*
saying you're grown up now,
You'd better be prepared for the real world,
because you've gotta make it somehow.
When your foundation from home is good,
that's an enhanced shot.
Being sheltered and unprepared for
turbulence or feeling entitled
Will introduce you to 'Mr. I think not',
next stop, *emotional shock.*

Yes you can be what you choose,
so much comes down to choice.
The decisions you make; will measure how you rejoice.
There will be rough days, great days and sad days too,
You just have to learn to be strong enough
To be able to face the truth.

Now if there's something that you didn't understand,
or this was a message that you just didn't get,
come see me in my office.
Class is dismissed.

Common Sense

I don't know if common sense is all that common.
I mean the definition says 'it's the ability to think and believe
in a reasonable way allowing you to make good decisions'.
However, when I look around and see the things
happening all over our country, I'm starting to think maybe
common sense is an idea that someone came up with
hoping everyone would join in on the conversation.

There are plenty of people I believe are on board, yet,
it's alarming to think of the number of those who are not.
I'm really concerned about our youth.
Their social skills are suspect in part because for many,
their primary method of communication
is an electronic device.
That's ok except for when it's time
to deal with live confrontation,
they're not prepared.
We can guide them but we can't always hold their hand,
sooner or later on their own emotional strength
they have to stand.
I was talking to a friend and she said,
"It's like when you first learned to ride a bike,
and it had training wheels". Soon with a little help
you learned to keep your balance, paddle straight,
you figured it out and you were on your way.
That's it! Maybe call it "figuring out Sense"?

Common sense can't be taught,
it's something that I believe is manifested
through intuitive reasoning.
Life and Situations are the Teachers.
Finding your own way out of difficulties
is a Process your Insight must feature.
Old school parents would always tell us
to 'act like we got some sense',
it's funny how decades later I truly understand
what that *profoundly simple statement meant*.
As smart as we think we are,
I feel too often it's others we try too hard to convince,
the game of life is full of bad plays,
it's amazing what could happen,
if we brought Common Sense off the bench.

Just a thought!

What Name Will You Answer To?

Long before you were called H's and B's you
carried a race and served as our Queen.
Women didn't feel the need to wear just
enough thread to call it a skirt,
Then get looser still to call it a shirt.
And then try to get mad at the wolves,
Because they're drooling over you like dessert.
Pulling down the elastic with every step you take,
trying to cover up your cookies before it's too late.
Really?

TV has suggested that's what you need to do,
To see anything or get a man you have to keep pace,
the more skin you show the less you have to wait.
Wrong!

Well I got news for you, for a lot of men,
it's never been about the length of your dress,
Because real men see more, when you show less.
It's ok to dress sexy yet classy, and show what you've got,
But if I can see everything baking in
your oven that outfit is too hot.

And then these fellas who are still sagging,
you telling me after all this time that's all you got
To signify you down, you tuff, and the baddest on the block?
If that's your thing then do what you do,
I'm not your parents, judge or anybody else who knows you.
But I'll tell you this, and this is for true,
They building prisons on the probability
that you'll be there soon.
I hope and pray that will never be your home,
But only you can decide,
if they got your future address wrong.

I don't know your situation, I don't know your circumstance,
But public education is free,
I'm just asking that you give it a chance.
Don't go just to pass the time or just to raise hell
Giving everybody a hard time and
making your presence smell.
I've been in those streets,
I've been in dark allies where I couldn't see,
I've been in places where death should have had me.

I know it's hard to see over those brick walls,
the pains of the chains won't let you answer the call
To your gifts, your talents and yes even your dreams.
But if you work hard enough, no matter how it seems,
it is possible, you can do anything,
I refuse to believe you don't want to be freed,
especially if you care to the extreme,
"No doubt" are the words your *willingness* must scream.

I'm not your preacher, I'm not your teacher,
I'm just a guy who made it out of the hood.
Sure there were some who didn't make it,
but we were all told a lot of us never would.
That doesn't have to be you, that doesn't have to be your fate.
We are the sum of the choices,
chances and opportunities we create.

I want you to make it, I want you to win,
it's gonna be hard but do whatever you can.
Don't worry about what other people say,
and you might have to break away from your crew;
And remember, it's not how they call your name,
but What You Answer To.

Peace Out!

Just A Thought...

A man who once lived in a car is now a billionaire.

A man lost his sight, was blind and vowed
to climb Mt. Everest and he did.

A woman cured years of drug addiction
by finding joy in running.

A man who was crushed by a bus, a broken body,
and wanted to die; had a change of heart and
completed an Iron Man race and finished a
26-mile marathon with three seconds to spare.

A woman of age swam the English Channel and
her only prize was to get to the other side.

A man who was given a 1% chance to live
with cerebral palsy, took his first
Steps at 25 years old.

I don't know your calamities,
maladies or what you are going through,
but if you can walk, talk, see and think,
what can you not do?
These people have demonstrated will beyond the unthinkable,
shown infinite faith that far exceeds the value of any treasure.
To see these things with my own eyes
more than inspires me to succeed,
I know anything is possible, if I truly believe.
...Your Move.

Time

As you read these words,
Seconds are going by,
They cannot be emulated,
No matter how hard we try.
Motion is constant, that is the
Nature of perpetual change.
Time is the paradox of opportunity,
too often squandered foolishly.

The fact that you're turning these pages,
allows your mind to be productive.
Learning is a building that should
continuously be constructed.

The world turns amid concerns.
Motivated and calculated,
How are you situated?
To accentuate this gift,
That cannot be manipulated.
That "Dash" in the middle of your Sunrise and Sunset,
determines if Time,
cheers the life 'you' defined.

CHAPTER 3

INTIMATE EXPRESSIONS

Sensuality permeates from the mind before its expressed in the physical. Words cannot only stimulate intellect, but they can also stir the senses beneath the covers of arousal. Let's ride the tide of passion, and delve into the bedroom of Intimate Expressions.

Can We Flow

Can I be your, Buffalo Chicken Wang,
Your Cookie Monster without fangs?
The Engine Engine Number Nine
Of your Supercalifragilisticexpialidocious Air Line.
I've been wanting to holla at you for some time,
But I only had 90 cents, I needed a dollar, and, you're a dime.
So, for real, for *sho*, can we flow?

Let me be the Houdini in your ooh wee.
The strawberries in your letter number 23.
The cayenne pepper in your nights of Kung POW,
That causes sweat to drip like waterfalls down your brow.

Nitro injections running through intersections
In a high speed chase to be the smile on your face.
Elemental and consensual,
I am equipped with the necessary essentials.
You can be my Wi-Fi and I'll be your electricity,
With googolplex capabilities to hot wire
your hot spots iniquities.
Sending effervescent surges via Micro Burst Frequencies,
Putting the wobble in your knees
and the sweetener in your cream cheese.
Will you let that be me?

The one who sets your stations
to unlimited purring destinations,
Like Time Warner Cable on Demand, I'll be your magic man.
Whatever you want, that's what you'll see
Because for you, I'd bankrupt eternity.
Let me be your Mai Tai, Your Cooley High,
The Lyrics in the Jackson 5's "Never Can Say Goodbye".

Can I take your cravings to the Outer Limits?
Fusing Parallel Realities causing abnormal faculties.
Sending your mind to the land of serene,
in my Magic Time Machine?
Or in your double Dutch bus, there will be only us.
You be my Porsche; I'll be your clutch.
So tell me baby, tell me quick,
Can you drive a stick?

I've been wanting to holla at you for some time,
But I only had 90 cents, I needed a dollar, and, you're a dime.
So, for real, for *sho*, can we flow?

Your Curves

There's something about a sexy woman with curves,
that summons invitingly naughty thoughts wrapped
around endless words. Thick thighs, luscious lips,
inner planetary waves from the switching of your hips.
Breasts that make me wanna rest
my head between those melons,
looking so scrumptious, I'm buying whatever you selling.
That plumpness of your chest, makes my hands start to sweat,
because I can't wait to have, what I wanna reach and grab.

I wanna sop you up like biscuits and gravy, cause ripples
across your sweetness, like I'm the Captain of your Navy.
Have you screaming in your dreams "Can you come here baby,
I need you right now to hurry up and save me".

Each woman is different, and those curves come in all sizes,
shapes and colors, but a sexy full figured woman
can bring it like no other. Your body is my playground,
inside your walls endless pleasures are found.
Confidence in who you are abounds,
because you and I both know,
you're the queen of putting it down.
Sexy, smart and sassy are just a few of your tagline words,
But what defines you most,
Is the power
In your curves.

Foreplay

I'm compelled to admit
Our session cannot hurriedly start
With a course of mere penetration
Without adequate lubrication
Stemming from the
Mental Masturbation
Your mind requires,
To produce the ultimate stimulation.

We put mundane to shame.
The latitude of our indulgence is insane.
I'm your Mr. Goodbar
You're my Almond Joy
We gave your rabbit radar,
And made your spot its toy.

It's the conversation that sets the stage
And tutors the roles played.
You'll be my nurse, I'll be your doctor
Let's bake your cookies
Tastier than a batch from
Betty Crocker.

It's the moisture between your ears
That relinquishes fears,
Allowing lubricious cheers to marinate infused restraint,
Releasing that woman in you that acts
out *all* her naughty pleasures,
And opens up the expressway lane to
your lascivious tunnels' treasure.

I feel you breathing,
I know what you're needing,
Exploratory expeditions,
That my tongue will be leading.

Chocolate Martini

Stir me slowly,
Allow the aroma of influence to sway you
unabatedly to my lever of pulsation.
Sip the intoxicant gently, as the warm cooling vibes
Saturate your inclinations, flowing effervescently,
Permitting your taste buds to savor the coco swirl,
Invigorating your arousals profusion,
As you inhale the succulent flavor,
Of my Chocolate Martinis' Sweetness.

Warm Up

Hello sexy,
I've been trying to reach you all day. I'm outside your office.
I know we're both busy but I had to call
and see if I could stop by
To tell you that I can't wait to see you tonight. Can I come up?
Wow, you look phenomenal.
I've been Imagining you at your desk, Me sliding underneath
Opening up your legs
And pealing back your dress.
You on the phone, fighting the fever of your moans,
Trying to handle your business
And your boss trying to figure out
Why are you breathing so heavily
While on his conference call;
Not knowing that I've launched your
Passion Fruit from your computer terminal to the hall.

Everyone leaves and heads to lunch,
I come from under your desk
I'm in the mood to hump.
You bend over your chair
It's the middle of the day
But we don't care.
You turn around, now I'm stroking you from the back,
your hands up against the glass,
hoping it doesn't crack because we wanna be bad,
Wetness pours down your back.
Looking out the window at the
People below, who have no idea
Your lustful volcano is about to blow,
if they looked up, they'd know
This sweltering encounter is just a prelim to our show.
I grab your hips we rock and then dip,
you knock your keyboard on the floor,
screaming deeper deeper!
More, more, more!
The office walls are now steaming,
Your nipples stand up like head lights beaming,
bursting from this fiery office scene, the juices of your
pleasure pearl erupt as the telephone starts to ring.
Your secretary asks are you alright.
You reply,
"Just warming up for tonight!"

Warm Sessions

Throughout the night, the warming of the flares
that burn in the furnace of our rapture,
will radiate with such bursts,
the flames will applaud the glow that's induced
by the fervor of our fiery excursion.

She Craves Me

It started with a call, an enthralling free fall,
Where voices were not enough
and face time was barren of touch.
Like an addict on the hunt for that thirst quenching hit,
Like a nymph lustfully urging a compulsively
copulating fever dripping fix.
Feeling my mouth bathing her from the top of her shoulder,
Down her neck then slowly smacking my
lips along the center of her back,
The codes that turn her on have been lusciously cracked.

Geometrically grinding, my grip binding,
massaging her round mound, her moans surfing sound
As my fingers prowl across the surface of
her inferno like invigorated cells,
Next stop her inner thighs where primal
waves are starting to swell.
Up to her nectarous juice pumping pearl,
Where restraint has opened the portal,
of her private orgy with an inviting sigh,
As desires gave way to the hunger that
makes her thermometers heat high.
She craves me

The walls of her sensual cave throbbing,
screaming, begging to misbehave.
Tossing, turning all over her bed, vigorously feeling
me expanding and positioning her legs,
Penetrating the deepest core of her hormones rage,
yearning to be conquered, released and slayed.
I take my arms and cradle her knees,
as morsels of sweat rain down like beads.
Her succulent nipples erect,
her hands eject from her valley so wet,
Her aphrodisiacal fluids had to be reset.
She craves me

Her breath is fading, her vision blurred
by her body's eruption,
Light turned upside down, her consciousness
on the verge of disruption.
The buildup, the tension,
mumbling words in search of diction.
Only I can feed her inextinguishable greed.
She is the fertility that has trademarked my seed,
Her love is the substance by which I bleed.

Screaming to be satiated, she couldn't wait any longer,
her cravings demanded that I salaciously fill,
Where no drop of my tastefulness will ever be spilled.
Her body is my oasis, flowing rivers to forbidden places,
Illicit dreams, vibrating themes, puddles from her quivers,
convulsion-like shivers,
Starving to receive the load I must deliver.
She craves me

The romp, the ride, the scorching highs,
as she calls my name while I rumble inside.
A Quake-like shake registering a 9.9, as the Hoover Dam
of her vaginal reservoir overflows one last time.

Then with an intensely moistened single stroke,
She traced upon her breast this sizzling note,
She craves me, and I replied.......
Her lust made me.

She Said... It's Been A Minute

He didn't ask for any details,
but the fire resonating from her eyes rivaled images of Zane's
steamy sexual romps in living color.

Her legs trembled as she closed them tightly,
fighting the hedonism
that begged her to lavishly spread her
lust ferociously over his stamina
and exhale her intense longing across the
table of her piping hot appetency.

She's ready; the walls of her sensual cave are an inferno.
Her skin feels like he's bare-handedly surfing over hot coals,
dispersing voluptuous cannons into the nucleus of her desire.
Her plum is ripe, she hungers delight,
She said, *"It's been a minute, so saddle up for the night."*

Heat

Every time I see you I want you.
My appetite for you
Is so unquenchable, searing and salacious;
The mere hint of you entertaining my whim,
Scorches the flirtation of our inseparability,
Sets a blaze to my salivating loins,
And uncoils the combustible tool
Of my kindled urge.

Love Potion

Turn down the night, its time to take flight,
On a magic carpet ride that defies all love highs.
You precede the idea of a notion,
for provocation permeates in your potion.
As tasty as a Cordial Cherry or an array
of unimaginable sweets,
I confess raw seductiveness kneels at your feet,
Because you leave my nature with no retreat.

Like the explosion of a voluptuous bomb
My nature clamors for your yum-yum
And every tantalizing curve of your body,
Is but a maze for me to enlist karate,
To fight back the avalanche of your mesmerizing appeal,
For within the contract of my soul,
You have sealed the deal.

Love Potion
I got it here come get it baby
Love Potion
Hurry up, don't keep me waiting.

Voodoo and scandalous clues, must be the tools
You skillfully use
To lure my senses to the fountains you choose,
To rain down tremors that tingle my skin
forbidding my unwillingness, to not be all in.

The turns that churn the angles that dangle.
Like Hades I yearn for your hellacious returns,
To enjoy so much, your ultra-hot touch,
These tides that roll, over the resistance you stole.

My atoms are intoxicated, molecules un-replicated,
Red blood cells now duplicated
As heat erupts and ignition is created.
And now for the climax, of all the commotion,

Are the drips, from your lips, I call love potion.

Overload

I wanna tune into your copulation station.
Dial the channels of metaphysical delectations.
Flip the switch that instantly connects,
the frequency of uninhibited dialects.
Upload my hard drive, into the aphrodisiacal
region of your main frame,
until the gigabytes required to process the data,
shut down the Internet of your brain.

Vibrations

I'm going to make your hormones hum,
like a European Engine on the German Autobahn.
Revving up the nectary of your felicitously palatable *Kitty*,
causing quivalation and welcoming your *Frisky*.
Strategically tuning up my *Tube* with your *Lube*,
100% High Octane, will be the *Grade*, of our *Fuel*.

*quivilation – the point where shivering and elation meet.

Bliss

Love is like music the way you use it.
Every melody in your sigh,
Creates a symphony in my eyes.

Like a conductor you masterfully control the flow,
As my baritone winds inhale you close,
At the precipice of your imperial arrangement,
On top your score rings, without containment.

The crescendo of your eighth note.
Eloquently peaks as your g-clef insatiably floats.
And the ambient light of our darkened room,
Sizzles as satisfaction is torridly consumed.
The moisture from our bodies shimmers
with hypnotic notions,
As our lyric sheet ignites the measure, of our titanic motions.

As the accent of your moans throb against my chest,
The pounding of our hearts rises before rest.
And as you quiver and shiver,
As a prelude to what pure passion sensually delivers.

Every ounce of my virility attentively stands,
To pay homage to the cascading touch of your hands,
As they traverse the terrain of my back with demand
For your finale,
To simmer, roar, explode and land.
Simmer, roar, explode and land.
Simmer, roar, explode and land.
Ahhhhh...

Now we sleep.

CHAPTER 4

UPLIFTING WORDS

Most of us aspire to be great and live in the hallways of success as we define it. How do we make a difference in the lives of others? Uplifting Words seeks to raise your spirit and encourage the drive in your aspirations, through the testimonials of one's perseverance to never give up or quit. Most of all, it is my hope that these passages leave you believing in the power of you and the fulfilling reward of persistence.

I Believe

When I look in the mirror I realize I am not inferior,
to those who boast of nothingness
and are not my souls' superior. I've made plans,
I've set goals, the difficulties I face,
My strength will control. I will not give in;
I will not back down.
Only I can overcome, the barriers of frowns.
Divine design has outlined my life,
with each fork in the road, I must choose right.
Knowledge and wisdom are my guides to find,
liberating discernment to nourish my mind.

My destiny lies within my hands. Steadfast in the
center of life's storms must I stand.
Because darkness cannot exist, in the power of light,
My path is made clearer by the plight of my fight.
Urgency is the fuel that propels my conduit,
My meeting with providence has a date attached to it.

My drive is anchored solely in the faith,
that as I run this race, fear has no place.
The wickedness of doubt has been replaced,
with unyielding vigor and undaunted haste.
With a burning desire to win and inspire,
for myself and others who yearn to live higher.
This is the legacy to which I'm compelled to aspire.

I will not be deterred, I will not be detained,
Victory is on a mantle, glistening on my name.
To this course, I'm purposely committed,
with platinum laced straps have my boots been fitted.
No excuses, it's up to me to put in the work,
Diligent and triumphant over the challenges I search.
Mere words will not bring to fruition,
this vision I've conceived,
My actions must mirror my mantra,
Without a doubt...

I Believe.

I Still Dream

I still dream of a day, when brothers of all colors
will stand united in support of one another.
Not for the glory of sport or in a battle
that an ideology has raged,
But within the prestige of righteousness,
Where revolutionary peace has turned the page.

Answer The Call

Life has chosen you to walk into its auditorium.
The audience, is Each Day.
The theater, is your Beliefs. The stage, is your Exemplification.

The agenda of your performance revolves
around how you express yourself.
The crowds will applaud the truth,
they will be entertained by your presence.
But more importantly, they will embrace you
when you show them the real you.
They will cheer unselfishness and revere morality.

Why? Because if your purpose is driven by
honesty and virtue, and the crowd feels you are real,
they will listen and follow you.
Not for the glamour of association or flashing bulbs,
but for the unpretentious manner
of your encouraging gesture.
Therefore, I implore you to believe
in something greater than yourself.
I'm not advocating one cause or another,
nor am I saying live to please everybody.
That premise borders the realm of impossibility;
but stand for something bigger than you.
Support a cause that you truly want to be a
part of that will facilitate changing lives.

Take a stand. That may not be who you are and you may
want to just take a casual stroll across the earth with a
carefree disposition. If that's what you choose to do with this
precious cycle of time called life, then so be it. I will never
judge you. Yet, if you desire more, I'm betting that when
you find what you were placed here to do and immerse
yourself in that nutriment, humanity will be better for it.

And at the end of your show, when the credits roll,
exalting your performance,
your engaging life and your impactful contributions,
the patrons will make known their gratification.
Your name will reign amongst those who made a difference,
as you witness and receive, a standing ovation.
Because you enhanced, the life of another.

Curtain Call!

Reach Higher

Do not dwell in the obscurity of mediocrity,
nor swim in the oceans of procrastination.
When you aspire higher, your destination
must exist beyond mere desire.
When you choose not to loose, you may not be first to start,
but your faith keeps you in the race.
Dedication to a goal well planned helps you keep pace.
Not quitting on you, and doing what's
necessary yields the dream you chase.
The relentless pursuit of persistence,
secures your destiny's date.

To My Nieces, Nephews And Grandchildren

Ok Listen up young kings and queens,
you know I'm not one for mincing words.
I just want you to understand, we're trying to
raise you right, the best that we can.
I know some of you are only six and headed to the first grade,
But for you to become men and women,
some ground rules have to be laid.

So when you grow up and look back on this talk
You'll recall these words and be thankful they weren't false.
Know you have to work hard, be strong and tough,
And learn quickly the rules don't always
apply to those who look like us!

But there's no excuse not to succeed,
make the right choice and then believe.
Don't be intimidated by bullies,
or be afraid to wear your hoodie,
Just know this before you begin,
what neighborhood you're in.
Don't go looking for a fight,
but stand up for what you feel is right.

I know some of you are only six and headed to the first grade,
But for you to become men and women,
some ground rules have to be laid.

Respect yourself, your elders and others and
most of the time they'll respect you,
Don't pay any attention to foolishness
just do what you gotta do.
Now I want you to study hard and get your education,
But books don't teach common sense that
gets you out of certain situations.
You have to know the game and recognize the system.
You gotta watch, learn and listen.

I'm telling you right now they're building prisons
based on you not passing some kind of test,
But a jail cell will not be your future home or your address.
If I have to beat you down to the ground to make you see,
That dungeon full of hopelessness is not where you wanna be.
This is real talk, because money is being
made based on you being a statistic.
This whole family and neighborhood are
gonna make sure you remain optimistic.

I know some of you are only six and headed to the first grade,
But for you to become men and women,
some ground rules have to be laid.

Observe where you are, look around,
get to know people who don't like to frown.
Enjoy being young but remember what you've been taught,
Don't let nobody own you and for no price be bought.
Don't listen to strangers, they're always full of danger!
And if someone crazy you don't know asks
do you wanna have some fun?
You get the hell out of there quick, don't walk, you run!
Then call Aunt Joyce and the whole family will come!

Tell the truth don't lie, keep your head up,
don't let them make you cry.
I'll be right here when you get out of school,
something ain't right, don't worry, it's cool.
Just let me know, I got your back, go do your thing,
now fist bump that!

Let Nobody Hold You Back

Don't hang your head or by perpetrators be misled.
Set your own pace.
Don't worry about the pack
Be meticulous in detail,
and let nobody hold you back!

Keep It Moving

I must remain focused.
I will not be intimidated by obstacles premeditated.
Nor shall I be derailed, by the frustrations of failures hell.
Each barrier obliterated is only a test,
I'm moving forward at a rate called 'My Best'!
Only at the podium of prestige shall I rest.
To re-tool the aspirations,
For my next Quest!

Fortitude

We must elevate above our disappointments,
be greater than our remorse,
Allow resilience to delineate our mental makeup
and wisdom discern our choice.

A Place Beyond Despair

"From The Journal Of A Survivor"

A strength without measure
To giving up you say 'never'.
When challenged by this robber of lives,
Hope told your spirit you will survive.

An unyielding belief, braced you for the news,
About a Battle you entered that you did not choose.
One that touches all of us, whose reach is worldwide,
Deep are the rivers of the many who've cried.

Here's to the families and all the friends,
Who share love faithfully with the prayers that they send.
To the caregivers and all the Inspirers of Hope,
To the Supporters, Runners and Walkers who race to cure,
One of life's bitter slopes.

For the tears and fears, and loved ones
we've lost, inside our years;
To the moments, when emotions erupted into cheers.
Because the letter of life came back saying,
no expiration date here.

For those days when you had to Endure
Yet another procedure or test;
For the nights you tossed and turned as sleep found little rest.

Here's to your Courage to say,
Although this Journey is an uphill plight,
You're never giving up on this precious gift called life,
You have the Faith, Determination,
The Will, and the Might; to proclaim this battle
Will be an Epic Fight! And when the bell rings,
To announce its end, there'll be no ashes,
scattered in the wind;
For your tomorrows have become, days without end.

For the Sunsets to come, for the Laughter
your heart has yet to see,
For the Joy in the midst of Euphoria,
When we all bask in the deliverance of being....

Cancer Free.

Unbroken

From the dungeons of purgatorial cells, rise you did,
From the chains of a tormenting hell.
Broken and battered, shattered in dust, in the light of life,
You lost all trust.

Then on the edge of a fallen cliff,
grace extended a passport to lift.
Back from oblivion and blurred osmosis,
fate is a friend yet favor is closest.

Gone were the haunting pillars of fire
that seduced imperfections
Like the cutting of barbed wire.
Like a Phoenix from the scattered ashes you rose,
For in your DNA majesty grows.

You were born for greatness; mountains rumble your name,
When you stepped into your purpose,
the Book Of Life changed.

Stand Tall

And though we proceed with caution
Our liberties cannot be auctioned.
Therefore, in the face of it all
We must unanimously stand tall!

And The Question Is?

We pray each day for the pain to go away.
Thoughts without wishes cut devoid of stitches;
Leaving scares that never fade,
as you cry out desperately to be saved.
Now empty screams emphatically search for hope,
Because the jail cells of life you now realize are no joke.
Swimming in a sea of disarray, you can barely float
On questions unanswered, so desperation throws you a rope.
Where are you now?

Some say do this, others say do that,
You no longer have the strength, because your *Will* is on flat.
You tried everything you thought you knew how to do;
Friends wouldn't click on the incoming call
So your message didn't get through.

Now at the brink and squarely at the break
Weary of the battles
And your options are running late;
Fear crept in and proposed an early life escape,
Yet something inside your deliverance, said fate can wait.
You entrusted your fortune in the hands of man,
When there is a power far greater,
That can do what no one else can.
Redemption and exemptions,
From whatever your regrets have to mention,
Leading you to a path, of righteous intentions.

Don't throw in the towel, all is not lost.
You've tried everything else
And found the remedies to be false,
For me I know what I would do;
I know the refuge of my first choice,
In Him I've inherited peace
As Love said, "Rejoice."
Time is ticking, seconds always find a way to come up missing.
With all that being said,
I implore you not to feel, this question is odd,
With so much at stake,
Have you ever, tried God?

Rejoice

Let's take this gloriously beautiful day and place it in a bottle,
so when the dark clouds and cold days appear,
we'll pop the cap and sprinkle a little sunshine,
when we need a ray of light to brighten our way,
bringing a smile, to uninvited moods.

Saved

Had *Love* not conjured its awakening within
the chords of my *Compassions* climate,
Charity would be oblivious,
Kindness would be void of *Tenderness*,
And prides' *Foolish Strength* would lay wasted,
on the island of *Never*.

Celebrated Lives

Innumerable prayers soar amongst
a multiplicity of supplications.
The space vacated by your company's aura will remain
within the vicinity of our lingering memories.
Some will express missing you with tears. Others with words
recollecting countless smiles originating from gestures
you brought about. Still many will drift into a place
only the circumference of the universe can encompass
for vast is the terrain of your enduring love.

Great is our loss. To say you'll be missed, humbly falls short
of the sentiments that beg to be poured out of cherished
vessels full of memories. Know that we will miss you.
More than that, we will celebrate you!
In every song that we sing together in happy times,
at every feast we prepare on holidays,
in every smile on the faces of those you left behind
that remind us of you and in conversations,
as we reminisce about all the wonderful things you would do.

Here's to the sunshine you brought to so many lives.
Here's to your loving spirit that touched us through your eyes,
with blessings and happiness that will always abide.
Here's to the imprint you left on our souls, that allows us
to have warms hearts, even though you've gone home.

Celebrated Lives

Ms. Shirley Marie Lynch
Mr. Yul LaMorton Lynch
Mr. Nelson Evans
Mr. John Dallas "JD" Goodman
Mr. Anthony "Andy" James Hawkins
Mr. & Mrs. Claude and Ramona McCain
Mrs. Viola Dickerson
Rev. Charles Drayton
Mrs. Kathy DeVaughn Mullins
Mr. Auswell Godwin
Mr. Cedric Howard
Dr. Jerome McNeil
Rev. Anthony Foster
Coach Ellis Davis
Mr. Michael Battle
Mr. & Mrs. Edgar and Ola Mae Lewis
Mr. Harold Hubbard
Mrs. Shirley Lassiter
Mrs. Gladys Mims
Mrs. Helen Johnson
Ms. Sandra Underwood
Mrs. Lottie Gray
Ms. Bridgett Taylor
Mr. Randle Jones
Mr. Barry Wooten
Mr. Charles Johnson
Mr. Darwin Bradford
Ms. Arnell Simmons
Ms. Caldine Montgomery
Ms. Gladys Russell
Mr. Dwayne Woods
Mr. Charles Lewis
Mr. Charles Aaron Gray
Mr. Jesse Lee Brown

Heroes

(A Salute To Our Men and Women Who Serve)

We don't always see and know what you do,
Yet in the trenches of night,
You shield and watch over us too.
Day in and Day out your lives are on the line,
Against all that threaten danger,
In the midst of peaceful times.

For the veterans who stood firmly and
for the soldiers we've lost,
So that we may walk in harmony, high is the cost.
For your service, your honor,
for every man, woman, boy and girl,
Great is your contribution, to save an unpredictable world.

For more than glory's sake you fight to liberate.
For in our country, democracy reigns,
And we must never take for granted
You who give up so much, your sacrifice, your pain;
So that we can walk our streets, devoid of change,
And the independence of a nations people, remains the same.

For the Army, Navy, Air Force and Marines
To the US Marshalls, ATF, the DEA,
and the Department Of Justice,
The keepers of constitutional dreams.
To the First Responders,
To the Guards, Special Forces, the Agents
and all who Protect and Serve,
To those behind the scenes and the accolades you deserve.

For the liberties you defend, for freedom without end,
We lift you up as we dance on life's unknowing wind.
There is no day that you are away from your post,
As your families pray you come home to a toast.
For your deeds we offer parades and a roast,
As you embrace the loved ones who care for you most.

I pray you know this is straight from the heart.
For the lives you save and protect,
Our Appreciation will never part.
We salute you today, and all that you do,
For the courage you display,
Protecting the Red, White and Blue.

A Mothers Love

There are no words to profess all that you've meant to me.
Incredible are the sacrifices that you gave,
in lieu of all your needs.
Unconditional love, a queen, mother above all nations,
What do these words really mean?
Not enough to embellish your imprint on my life,
Down to the very little things.

You are my mother. So much is amplified
just by saying those words.
Your voice in troubled times, can be encouragingly heard.
You implanted in me, your work ethic,
and you made sure respect wouldn't be neglected.
For the nights you stayed up when I was sick,
to make sure that I could sleep.
For the dedication to raising and protecting your children,
And how you saved us from the streets.

For the dinners on Sundays, the feasts on holidays.
For making a way, when all seemed lost,
With no hesitation in paying whatever the price,
Unimaginable was your cost.

For all the times you were cleaning the house
Even when your body was in pain,
You never failed in caring for us all,
through the sunshine and the rain.
In all my living I've come to discover,
How supreme is the connection to the Love of Your Mother!

I remember you getting up at 4:00 AM preparing
us for school, our breakfast and lunch.
Riding the bus, working two and three jobs
just so our family had enough.
There will never be a way to repay you for all you've done,
And I'm so sorry I didn't get a chance to
do what I could do for you now,
Before the setting of your evening sun.

This is for you my mother, and for all mothers,
Those who are here now, and for those who've gone home,
For the many who shed silent tears,
because The Heart of Their Life, is the story of sad songs.
I cherish you, we cherish you and miss the joy of your smile,
Just to hear your voice on the phone was a pleasure
When we would sit and chat for a while.

From all that you gave and the prayers you prayed,
To how you could take bad times and make hardship behave.
This is for you and all the accolades you deserve
For filling our appetite with wisdom and the
hunger of belonging that you curved.

Here's to a billion words, soaring on the wings of doves,
Searching to find thoughts to encompass,
The Preciousness
Of
A Mothers Love

A Fathers Holiday

When you are a father, you are the man,
You provide the strength
For those too weary to stand.

For your faith and for your devotion,
For your family, you put love in motion.
For all that you give, every single day,
For those you encourage and the tears you wipe away.

This is your moment, it is your time,
We celebrate who and all that you are,
Your legacy will live forever,
Beyond times farthest star.

Here is the gift, that expresses the feelings
That unwritten words simply can't say,
To sum up what you mean to us,
Each and every day.

For all that you share and help us through,
Your dedication always remains true.
And for the many times you've led the way,
With love and adoration, we give to you,
A Fathers Holiday.

A Courageous Step

Walking away is never easy when binding rivers of
familiarity flow through the vessels of solitary images.
It is the fear of being alone that stands in
the doorway of reality revealed.

That lying truth, camouflaged by falsely deserving abuse,
Can only be rescued by fortified nerves,
arriving as lifesaving troops.
And that chamber of isolation that now holds you prisoner,
Has no right to your life, with or without a signature.

How is living in the bondage of discontentment more
appealing than a room filled with voices of why?
The courage to leave is difficult, the option to stay
is a rope tied with knots of guilt whose merit
is irreverent when measured against your peace of mind,
well-being and the structure of your self-esteem.

You can do better, be better, live and sleep better,
without being tucked in by tears
who desperately cry for their escape.
Help is begging for a call, realizing so much is at stake.

Don't let enough be a destination you arrive at too late.
Choose departure, and only you can drive
the vehicle of freedom to that station.
Get there and a haven of restfulness awaits your strength
which cut the strings of your unhappiness.
Be strong, and don't hold on to anything or anyone
That does not want to hold you.
Somehow some way,
Find the courage,
To walk away.

Joy

Deploy your joy when you walk into a room.
It cannot be taken nor indiscriminately consumed.
You're in control, Joy encompasses your soul. It's up to you!
Don't let the world break through!

Don't Give Up

No matter what you're going through
And especially when times get tough,
Remember these words,
Don't give up!

Broken hearted, body torn with only lint in your pocket,
You're tired, no where to lay your head or find peace,
And your life, has no socket.

You must have faith,
Keep your head to the sky.
The suns rays will break through the haze,
And they will carry you by and by.

Defeat is temporary, but only if you don't quit.
Don't give in to self pity, self doubt has no measurement.
When the hour seems the darkest and there is nothing left,
Journey to that place of validation,
Called 'I must believe in myself'.

No matter what you're going through,
And especially when times get tough,
Remember these words,
Don't give up!

Free your heart and strengthen your mind
And you will know all in good time,
Your plan that was written by the Divine,
But you have to stay the course,
For that rainbow to shine.

Be strong for your family, be strong for you,
I know it's hard when you're lonely,
but every day you wake up
It's a blessing and another chance
To make dreams come true.

No matter what you're going through,
And especially when times get tough,
Remember these words,
Don't give up!

You Can Do It

We have to talk,
I want you to know I believe in you.
But more importantly,
I need you to believe in you too.

You can't wish to be redeemed
Chase hollow schemes,
Not tirelessly spread your wings,
And expect to achieve uncommon things.

There's no lottery ticket to winning.
Even a jackpot requires a dollar just for a chance to play,
How about having your bio read,
You won the trophy by getting the most out of every day.

Stop talking about what you're going to do.
Just do what you're talking about!
That's the only way to cast that demon of *Why Not Me* out.

Get up, do it now, no more half-hearted efforts,
There're no promises for tomorrow,
Stop blaming your future,
On yesterdays sorrow.

You can do it, You can do it,
But it has to be a *Magnificent Obsession*,
Monuments of Consistency
Have to be the Railway of your Direction.
You have to want it so bad,
The arteries of your Subsistence
Shall bear your flag.

Here's the plan, here's how we get this done;
Make every second count and not half-step on a single one.
Lay the course and from intrepid commitment never divorce.
I'll meet you at the finish line,
As you put to rest the questions of *What* and *How*,
Step on the platform of Triumph,
And then, take your bow!

I Dare You

Ok enough with the 'I'm living a hard life and I'm
stuck in this hole and I ain't got no way out talk'.
You can't help where you were born; ok I give you that.
But that old adage 'it's not how you start but how you
finish' is true. And yes that means for you too.

And for the record, you're talking to a guy who was
raised by a single parent, My Mother! I know the taste
of powdered milk and eggs. Food Stamps with rent that
was 65 dollars a month for a three bedroom apartment.
Where do you think that penthouse was? Lunch tickets
and bus cards and yes I paid a nickel for a transfer to
get to the other side of town to get down. But through
it all, I didn't drown in some pity party for myself.
I made a lot of mistakes and grew from each pitfall.
Most of all, I never stopped Believing.

Believing in what you say? I'm glad you asked.
"That it's not always gonna be this way!"
I was smart, athletic and creative. In other words
I was blessed. You too have something in you
that makes you special. You have a talent.
Find it! Believe it! Live it!
And most of all Never lose Hope in it!

I want you to grow, prosper and not stay in that
desolate place you call 'just getting by'.
That's not where you were meant to be.
That's a lie you've lived and allowed
to be the yoke of your discontent.
I'm not judging you. Never that. I have no right.
I'm just asking you to Step It Up.
I dare you to believe. I double dare
you to try with all you've got.
I triple dare you to draw your own road map.
Daily, gauge every incremental meter
towards Accomplishment.
Plan it, Command it and most Assuredly Stand in it.

I Dare You!

What If

What if there were no barriers,
Pernicious Bars or restrictions to impede your ascent?

What if nothing or no one hand cuffed your insistence?
You were free to crack the code to competency,
And not just settle for what you could get?
What if, It Was All On You?

Would you be the promise of your potential and
without reservation do what is essential
To obtain the credentials, that validate your
arrival to the summit of your aspirations?

When you look in the mirror,
are you happy with what you see?
If not, only your actions can change the
reflection to what you want it to be.
Not by making shallow resolutions,
But by being consistent in the follow through
of real practical solutions.

What if I told you, until you indict your
excuses and adopt the paradigm of
Leaving Nothing On, that Proverbial Table,
You might as well throw self-betterment
over the edge of a cliff.
Because until you squash the fallacies of Fear and Not Trying,
You'll tarry in the dungeon of What If!

Expect Success

We cannot know the outcome of an event before the end of its term. However, we can prepare expectedly, fully anticipating the fruits of our relentless pursuit from the culmination of our committed efforts, be resplendently rewarded.

Now

Because *My Future* has examined what *My Past* has rendered,
Now, has volunteered, to redefine both.

Perseverance

I cannot dwell in the dungeons of mediocrity
and expect to reach heights of prosperity.
I have to put in the work.
The plan must be followed to the hilt.
On the foundation of persistence, shall my Legacy be built.
I will not be shackled by *Excusable*
prerequisites or empty regrets.
The best chapters of my life have not been written yet.

Arrival

I do not measure myself against what
the world says I should be.
My bar of accomplishment resides inside
my willpower and self-discipline.
It ascends based on the performance of my actions
and the propelling of my potentials' actuality.

When I look into the mirror and without question, can say,
That I've exhausted every strand of my gift and ability,
Gave with integrity and determination all that was
necessary to finish my vision triumphantly,
and encouraged others to raise their level of acceptance,
Thus positively impacting their lives,
then and only then, will I grade the level of my success.

Purpose

Do you know why you're here?
Have you looked inside the curiosity of
your existence and asked yourself,
What sets you apart from those who win or lose?
Is preference the only reference for
what you arbitrarily choose?

One of the greatest 'ah hah' moments in life,
Is when we come to know the hand we'll use to write.
Then comes an affinity, from the back drops of anonymity,
An emergence of a skill, that is but a whim of your will.

Therefore, the Awakening and Deployment of that ability
Is ultimately our responsibility.
It's on us to connect the dots of lifes continuity.
The question then is no longer why we came to be,
But will you bring to the surface,
The complete realization of your Purpose?

Shine On

Hold On, Be Strong
March On, Shine On

We have marched the march and we've sung the hymns,
fought for the right to vote and the omission
of our voice we've condemned.
A man of color, has brilliantly become
the leader of the free world,
and from his vision has the liberty of freedom,
been gracefully unfurled.
Nonetheless, we have to remain entrenched
in the work not yet done,
diligent in our objectives, until we leave behind none.

Petitions will be submitted until our color is acquitted.
Not with some noisy ruckus,
but with strategy and cohesiveness among us.
Not with a banner of violence that leads
down battered and broken roads,
but with the vigor of expectations shall our ideals be sold.

We will make the grades, treasure young
lives saved, and pick up the slack,
where hope needs a way back.
On the field, on the stage, in the classroom
where bricks of knowledge are laid.
Through science and math, by teaching and learning,
as we feed young minds eagerly yearning.
Yet let us not forget, the preponderance of politics.
We cannot be indifferent but rather insistent.
If we want to say "in with the new" and "out with the old",
voting insists, we all get on board.
Be informed, then head to the polls,
that's one sure way change will take hold.
And when the storms of adversity come,
we'll keep pressing until our assignments right all wrongs.
So we Hold On, Be Strong, March On and Shine On.
We Hold On, Be Strong, March On and Shine On.

Let the haters hate who can't create, jealous because
your stardom, has a predetermined date.
Come what may, from your Objectives never stray.
And when the madness of sadness suddenly appears,
know in your heart there will be cheers,
For on the other side of the difficulties, joy trumps tears.
So do your thing, do it strong, and remember
to let your shine, always Shine On.
Keep on smiling it will carry you home,
And let your shine, always Shine On.

How?

We Hold On, Be strong, March On and Shine On.
Just Hold On, Be strong, March On and Shine On.
We Hold On, Be strong, March On and Shine On.
We Hold On, Be strong, March On and Shine On.

I Am Relevant

I looked up to the heavens,
and as the clouds shaped the Mural of my life;
blinding streets of gold,
poured out purity, that gave the day its light.
And then sirens of songs, like vessels of radiance,
pierced my soul. Glory called my name, and said,
"Stand and behold." I bowed to pay homage,
to His imperial benevolence; then in that moment of clarity,
I realized, I was surely relevant...

Covered

May you always have Faith, walk in the footsteps of Favor,
Be abundantly Blessed and showered by Grace.

Legacy

When you stand at the podium of life's
cumulative accomplishments,
have attained more than a modicum of
society's impression of success,
how will you measure all you've personally achieved,
against how you touched those who had less?

It is not by happenstance that you are here.
Before the overture of your corporeality,
a gift was planted within the fertile soil of your purpose.
A plan was foretold on the scrolls of destinies
arrivals amid the gathering of providence.
A plan was designed and when you're aligned,
the pathway to supernal heights
shall infuse downtrodden faces, with elevating light.

Audaciously plow a path for others to
walk in the future of their past.
What you do for yourself, leaves nothing left.
Yet all that you give, eternally lives.
In the dreams unseen through the window of realization,
through voices that speak to doubt
without fear of provocation.

Guide those who travel roads of confidence lacking,
lead them to the highway that sends failure packing.
And when they're not sure,
because the sign ahead says, "Detour;"
instill in their will not to be afraid,
For every wrong turn taken, another lane of wisdom is paved.

Give for no special reason in and out of season.
Deliberate in your gestures, arrogance sequestered.
Money alone is not enough,
it's detachment from the dollars' destination that
Often implies being out of touch.
It's your smile, your hand, that look of hope
you transfer to another's eyes,
Inspiring them to believe again, from the ashes they rise.

Therefore run with the wind,
ballet in the illumination of a crescent moon,
celebrate each rising of the sun, then toast to the
preciousness of life and what your merit has done.
Honor always those you hold dear,
in the inheritance of your labor let their ambitions cheer.
What you present to them now,
what you've bestowed when you're no longer here,
impacting generations to come,
on how their place in history can be won.
Let all that share your ideals,
and those you've paroled from despair,
exalt reciprocity, rewarding your dare
to lift broken spirits you committed to repair.

In quiet times and radiant rhymes the story of your relevance
will resound within the archives of all mankind.
Appreciative of the glory, yet humbly accepting the applause,
directing attention to the deeds,
insuring the integrity of the actions not be flawed.
Reflecting on the wonderment
atop the pedestal of triumph and achievement,
steadfast in your convictions, in deference and credence.

You ran the race with haste,
unbiased to those unable to keep the pace.
You did the unfathomable,
your contributions to others incalculable.
The transcriptions of those who shall expound to the scribes,
will tell how you made a difference in their lives,
while invigorating young minds.
Let the register of benevolence emphatically proclaim
for the entire world to see, that purpose with gracious intent,
was the hallmark, of your Legacy!

ABOUT THE AUTHOR

Zemill began his journey in the world of writing many years ago. With his sophomore book *Love Unleashed - The Fire and Passion of Poetry* and his second musical CD *Timeless - A Jazzy Poetic R&B Ride*, he is now passionately pursuing what he feels he was born to do, which is to "create lyrical images".

Born in Dallas, Tx and a graduate of Franklin D. Roosevelt High School and Southern Methodist University, where he earned a degree in Economics, Zemill was a gifted athlete and student. He gave up sports to work in Corporate America where he has become a successful and well respected manager at the largest Transportation Company in the world.

A tireless man of vision and resilience he states his ultimate goal is, "to make a difference in the lives of his family, loved ones and in the world". A renaissance man, and award winning author, he continues to use his gift to excite, entertain and stimulate the mind, body and soul. His upcoming projects include movies, TV Shows, plays, merchandising and several more books are in the pipeline. Zemill is currently promoting his highly alluring and engaging *"PoJazz Experience"* where he blends Smooth Jazz, Smooth R&B, and Lyrical Poetry to create an incredibly mellow ride of rhythmic vibrations. He continues to be a man on a mission!

"Zemill's ability to express beautiful thoughts is amazing!"

--David A. Small
Entertainment Attorney

"Zemill is talented, with an impeccable work ethic!"

--Cheryl Smith
Newspaper and Magazine Publisher

"Zemill is an artist who can take the art of poetry and set it to a beat, cause rhythm to rhyme and move to the cadence of words."

--Sharon Banks
Twin Cities Radio Network

"Absolutely charming. Modern day Shakespeare".

--Di Moore
Dallas

"Zemill takes you on an emotional roller coaster ride that taps into the essence of your spirit. His words are thought provoking yet inspiring. One minute you feel empowered and proud and the next minute you're filled with desire and curiosity. He takes you on a journey down memory lane that can fill you with tears of sorrow or joy and leaves you wanting more."

Dr. Lawana Gladney
Emotional Wellness & Mind Doctor

"You are amazing in what you create and deliver. Love It!"

--Lady Ladonna

"It's been said that communication is not what you say but what people hear. Zemill has the ear of his audience and what they hear is excellence "In The Mix".

Jimmy Miller
Music Producer, Musician, Songwriter & Arranger

Unleashed

You extended clemency
to my hesitancy and
introduced opulence
to our intimacy.
Replaced insatiable, unconfined lust,
brought to the Surface
Unequivocal Trust.
Paroled a wayward soul
whose emotions and introversions struggled to be controlled.
Exonerated feelings, imprisoned by an encrypted solitude
Chance professed, would never be released;
You tapped into a source that insistently propelled,
love to become...

Unleashed

Printed in the United States
By Bookmasters